RUSSIAN FOR LIBRARIANS

RUSSIAN FOR LIBRARIANS

G P M WALKER MA ALA

Slavonic and East European Section
Bodleian Library, Oxford

CLIVE BINGLEY  LONDON

FIRST PUBLISHED 1973 BY CLIVE BINGLEY LTD
16 PEMBRIDGE ROAD LONDON W11
SET IN 10 ON 13 POINT PRESS ROMAN
AND PRINTED BY LITHOGRAPHY IN UK
BY STEPHEN AUSTIN AND SONS LTD
COPYRIGHT © G P M WALKER 1973
ALL RIGHTS RESERVED
0 85157 156 5

TO ANNE

CONTENTS

INTRODUCTION

This book is intended for library and information staff who need to work efficiently with Russian-language material as part of the routine handling of their collections, but who are not concerned with selection or analysis of the material at a level which demands any considerable knowledge of Russian. It contains:

1. A short self-instructional course to supply a highly limited and specialised Russian vocabulary and grammar. This is planned to make possible the identification of documents in Russian; their handling in acquisition routines, simple cataloguing, classification and serial records; and the consultation of basic reference works.

Notes on:

2. Transliteration systems and practices.

3. Cataloguing problems: bibliographical peculiarities of Soviet publications.

4. Reference works: current Soviet bibliographies, other sources of bibliographic data for Russian-language material, quick-reference works in English on Russia and the USSR, and Russian-English dictionaries.

5. Acquisition of Russian publications.

6. Identification of other East European languages.

and:

7. Russian-English vocabularies.

This is, as far as I know, the first such work intended for English-speaking librarians. It is based on courses run for staff at the University of Lancaster Library, to whom I am grateful for pointing out deficiencies. Use by individual learners is a very different matter, however, and comments on the content and presentation of the book will be very welcome. They should be sent to the author at the Slavonic and East European Section, Bodleian Library, Oxford OX1 3BG.

SEPTEMBER 1972   GPMW

ABBREVIATIONS

acc.	accusative case
adj.	adjective
adv.	adverb
dat.	dative case
fem.	feminine gender
gen.	genitive case
instr.	instrumental case
ipfve	imperfective aspect
loc.	locative case
masc.	masculine gender
neut.	neuter gender
nom.	nominative case
pfve	perfective aspect
pl.	plural
prep.	preposition
sing., sg.	singular

1. RUSSIAN COURSE

1.1. LEARNING RUSSIAN

Although Russian is, in terms of its history and structure as a language, related relatively closely to English and to other West European languages, it has unfamiliar features which make it more difficult to learn than, say, German or Spanish for most native English speakers. Although this book is intended only for a limited and specialised study of the language, it will nevertheless introduce the learner to, and give him practice in, a number of these unfamiliar characteristics.

The Cyrillic alphabet, in which Russian is written, will probably not prove to be the great obstacle it seems at first sight. A number of the letters are similar to their equivalents in the Roman alphabet (although a few misleading resemblances must be watched for), and others closely resemble letters of the Greek alphabet. An advantage over English is that written Russian gives a much better — though not perfect — indication of its pronunciation: the sound or sounds associated with each letter of the alphabet are regular enough in occurrence to make a comprehensible pronunciation possible by following a minimum of rules. Throughout this course, the exercises should be treated as practice in spelling out, reading and writing Russian, and at a later stage transliterating it into Roman characters.

The structure of Russian makes much greater use than English of variations in word-ending to show differences in the grammatical usage of a word. The notion of gender ('masculine'/'feminine'/'neuter') plays as important a part in Russian as it does in German or Latin, and is likewise reflected in word-endings. These sets of endings ('declensions') are treated here in some detail for Russian nouns, adjectives and pronouns, since their accurate recognition is often important in, for example, the correct citation of an author's name or the understanding of a title-page.

The complications of Russian verb usage, which would need to be tackled at length in acquiring a good general knowledge of Russian, have in this course only been outlined: verbal constructions are much less significant than normal in the variety of Russian met with in simple document handling.

The vocabulary of Russian, again, has fewer obvious points of contact with English than the vocabularies of West European languages, calling perhaps for a rather greater effort of memory. However, this course sets out to give a 'passive' knowledge — that is, the ability to translate in the Russian-to-English direction only — using a strictly limited set of words and phrases, with exercises and examples to show their use in context.

In working through the course, the vocabularies and exercises given at intervals should be taken unhurriedly and at length by those needing anything more than a nodding acquaintance with the appearance and character of Russian. *Wherever possible, further original material in Russian should be used for close examination and extra practice. Skill will come only with practical experience.*

1.2. ALPHABET, SCRIPT, PRONUNCIATION

1.2.1. Alphabet. The Cyrillic alphabet as used in Russian now consists of 32 letters in the order shown below:

Printed cap/lc	Script cap/lc	Name of letter (approx Anglicised)	Approx pronunci- ation	Examples	
А а	*Ѧ а*	ah	*a*rc	а	and, but
				автор	author
Б б	*Ѣ б*	beh	*b*ed	без	without
В в	*В в*	veh	*v*an	век	century
Г г	*Г г*	geh	*g*as	год	year
Д д	*Д д*	deh	*d*ot	до	until
Е е	*Е е*	yeh	*y*et	все	all
Ё ё	*Ё ё*	yo	*y*ore	её	her, hers
(usually written E, e)					
Ж ж	*Ж ж*	zheh	vi*si*on	жизнь	life
З з	*З з*	zeh	*z*one	закон	law
И и	*И и*	ee	*vi*sa	и	and
				из	from
Й й	*Й й*	ee kratkoye ('short ee')	co*i*n	май	May
				война	war

14

Printed cap/lc	Script cap/lc	Name of letter (approx Anglicised)	Approx pronunciation	Examples	
К к	*Ӄ ӄ*	kah	*k*id	как	how
				книга	book
Л л	*Л,л*	el	woo*l*	глава	chapter, head
М м	*Мм.*	em	*m*ap	Москва	Moscow
Н н	*Жн*	en	*n*ow	не	not
О о	*О о-*	oh	*o*re	от	from
П п	*П п*	peh	*p*ot	под	under
Р р	*Рр*	ehr	ki*r*k (Scots)	роман	novel
				редактор	editor
С с	*С с*	ess	*s*ea	собрание	collection
				страна	country
Т т	*Т,т,т,т*	teh	*t*on	театр	theatre
				том	volume
У у	*Уу*	ooh	r*u*le	университет	university
				Украина	Ukraine
Ф ф	*Фф*	eff	*f*at	физика	physics
Х х	*Хх*	kha	lo*ch*	художник	artist
Ц ц	*Цц*	tseh	cur*ts*ey	цена	price
Ч ч	*Ч ч*	cheh	*ch*eek	что (pron. што)	what
				человек	person
Ш ш	*Ш ш.ш*	shah	*sh*ot	школа	school
Щ щ	*Щ щ*	shchah	pu*sh-ch*air	ещё	still, yet
ъ	*ъ*	tvyordy znak – see 1.2.2. ('hard sign')			
ы	*ы*	yer*ý*	wh*i*sky (Scots)	мы	we
ь	*ь*	myakhki znak – see 1.2.2. ('soft sign')			
Э э	*Ээ*	eh	*e*nd	эра	era
Ю ю	*Ю ю*	yu	*yu*le	юг	south
Я я	*Я я*	yah	*ya*rn	я	I
				язык	language

The use of the following letters was discontinued in the Soviet Union in 1918, but they continued to appear in émigré publications for many years:

i	i	i	*i*	ee	v*i*sa	(now replaced by и)
Ѣ	ѣ	*Ѣ*	*ѣ*	yat'	*y*et	(now replaced by е)
Ѳ	ѳ	*Ѳ*	*ѳ*	feeta	*f*at	(now replaced by ф)
V	v	*Ѵ*	*ѵ*	izhitsa	v*i*sa	(now replaced by и)

1.2.2. 'Hard' and 'soft' signs. ъ and ь indicate variations in the pronunciation of the preceding sound or sounds. ь indicates a 'palatalisation', which can often be roughly reproduced by inserting a slight -y- sound, *eg:*

ть has about the quality of *t* in *t*ube: быть   to be
нь „   „   „   „   „ *n* in *n*ew: жизнь   life
сь „   „   „   „   „ *s* in He*ss*ian: письмо   letter

ъ is now only occasionally used, to show the absence of a 'palatalisation' where it might otherwise be expected. Until 1917, however, it was regularly used, though not pronounced, at the end of all words not ending in a vowel or the 'soft sign', *eg* отъ (now от), годъ (now год).

1.2.3. Learning the alphabet. Notice that:
1. These letters are *usefully* similar to English letters in pronunciation:
А Б (=b) Д (=d) Е З (=z) К М О С(=s) Т Э (=e)
2. These are *misleadingly* similar to English letters:
В (=v *not* B) И (=i *not* N) Н (=N *not* H) Р (=R *not* P) У (=U *not* y)
Х (=kh *not* x) ъ and ь ('hard' and 'soft' signs, *not* b) ы (short i, one sound only, nothing to do with ь or b) Я (=ya *not* R)
3. These letters are usefully similar to Greek:
Г (=g) Д (=d) Л (=L) П (=p) Р (=r) Ф (=f)
4. Learn to distinguish between these groups:
– б (=b), в (=v), р (=r), ъ ('hard sign'), ь ('soft sign'), ы (short i), ѣ (pre-1918, =e).
– ж (=zh), х (=kh).
– л (=L), п (=p), ц (=ts), ч (=ch), ш(=sh), щ(=shch).
– у (=u), ч (=ch).

1.2.4. Script. The examples below show the method of joining letters in cursive script. Note that the italic type faces (examples shown later in the book) resemble written Cyrillic closely.

почта,
почта } почта post (=mail)   *имени* имени named

большевик   большевик Bolshevik

Ленинград   Ленинград Leningrad

библиография   библиография bibliography

должно быть
должно быть }   должно быть should be

сельскохозяйственный   сельскохозяйственный agricultural

отъ *редакціи* отъ редакціи   from the editors (pre-1918)

от *редакции* от редакции   „   „   „   (post-1918)

въ *Европѣ* въ Европѣ   in Europe (pre-1918)

в *Европе* в Европе   „   „   (post-1918)

EXERCISES 1
Print out and write in script all the Russian words introduced so far and arrange them in *Russian* alphabetical order, covering up the key below (as in subsequent exercises) until you give up.

а	and, but	ещё	still, yet
автор	author	жизнь	life
без	without	закон	law
библиография	bibliography	и	and
большевик	Bolshevik	из	from, out of
быть	to be	имени	named
в	in, into	как	how
век	century, age	книга	book
война	war	Ленинград	Leningrad
все	all	май	May
глава	chapter	Москва	Moscow
год	year	мы	we
до	until, up to	не	not
должно быть	should be	от	from, away from
Европа	Europe	письмо	letter
её	her(s)	под	under

17

полный	full	Украина	Ukraine
почта	post	университет	university
редактор	editor	физика	physics
редакция	editorship, editorial staff	художник	artist
		цена	price
роман	novel	человек	person
сельскохозяй-ственный	agricultural	что	what
		школа	school
собрание	collection	эра	era
страна	country	юг	south
театр	theatre	я	I
том	volume	язык	language

1.2.5. Stress. Pronunciation in general. The stressed syllable in Russian varies from word to word as in English, and also from one form of the same word to another, *eg* in the different persons of a verb conjugation. The pronunciation of unstressed vowels is often much slackened or slurred. Unstressed o, for example, is frequently sounded very like a.

For library use, it is not vital to know the stress pattern of Russian words, but it should be borne in mind that the 'correct' pronunciation — heard, say, over the telephone — máy sound rather different from what you expect, if you have seen a word only in print, with no stress indication. Accurate pronunciation demands more work (particularly with experienced speakers, records or tapes) than this book can provide: be prepared to speak slowly and distinctly, following the approximate pronunciation shown in 1.2.1, and to spell words out whenever necessary, preferably using the Russian names of Cyrillic letters.

1.3. ARTICLES. GENDER AND CASE

1.3.1. Articles. There are no definite or indefinite articles in Russian. книга may need to be translated as '*the* book', '*a* book', or simply 'book', according to the context.

1.3.2. Gender. Russian nouns are classified into masculine, feminine and neuter *genders,* with gender usually determined by the ending of the word.

18

Masculine are nouns ending in a consonant: лист 'leaf, sheet', конец 'end'.

nouns ending in -й: музей 'museum', Китай 'China'.

some nouns ending in -ь: словарь 'dictionary', читатель 'reader'.

Feminine are nouns ending in -а: газета 'newspaper', наука 'science, scholarship'.

nouns ending in -я: поэзия 'poetry', партия 'party'.

most nouns ending in -ь: печать 'press'.

Neuter are nouns ending in -о: слово 'word', издательство 'publishing-house'.

nouns ending in -е: введение 'introduction', сочинение 'work, composition'.

a few nouns ending in -мя: время 'time'.

EXERCISES 2

As with Exercises 1, print out, write in script and arrange in Russian alphabetical order words introduced since that point.

введение	introduction	печать	press
издательство	publishing-house	поэзия	poetry
Китай	China	словарь	dictionary
конец	end	слово	word
лист	leaf, sheet	сочинение	work, composition
наука	science, scholarship	читатель	reader
партия	party (in Soviet contexts, usually the Communist Party of the Soviet Union)		

1.3.3. Case. Russian nouns, adjectives and pronouns occur in six *case* forms according to their grammatical function, as in Latin and, to a lesser extent, German. The use of each is illustrated below.

Nominative: the case of the subject of a sentence, regarded as the 'standard' form and hence that shown in, for example, dictionary entries.

'*Книжная летопись*' издается с 1907 года.
'*Book chronicle*' has been published since the year 1907.

следующие книги вышли из печати.
The following books have gone out from the press [*ie* been published].

Accusative: the case of the direct object of a sentence. Also used after some prepositions.

Перевод с английского подготовил Л. С. Павлов.

[The] *translation* from English prepared L. S. Pavlov. (Note the inversion of the usual English word order here, made possible – apart from the sense, as here – by the use of word *form* instead of word *order* to show grammatical function.)

Genitive: The case showing possession ('whose?' or 'of what?'). Also used after many prepositions. In both functions very frequently met in document handling.

День *поэзии.*

[the] Day *of Poetry* (gen. sing. of поэзия).

собрание *сочинений.*

collection *of works* (gen. pl. of сочинение).

план *выпуска литературы.*

plan *of issue of literature* (*ie* 'forthcoming titles'. Gen. sing. of выпуск and литература).

резюме *статей.*

summary *of articles* (gen. pl. of статья).

от начала до конца

from beginning to end (both preps take genitive. Gen. sing. of начало and конец respectively).

Dative: the case of the indirect object ('to whom?' or 'to what?'). Also used after a few prepositions.

вся власть *Советам!*

all power *to the Soviets*! (dat. pl. of Совет).

приложение к *журналу*

supplement *to [the] journal.* (к takes dative. Dat. sing. of журнал).

Instrumental: the case of the instrument or agent ('by whom?', 'by what?'). Also used after some prepositions.

сборник составлен *коллективом*

[the] symposium [is/was] compiled *by a collective.* (Instr. sing. of коллектив. Note that the present tense of the Russian verb 'to be' is usually omitted. Despite the consequent telegraphic appearance, the sense of what remains is normally clear.)

20

Locative (or Prepositional): used only after a small number of prepositions, some of which indicate position and all of which are common, *eg* о 'about'; на 'on, in'; в 'in'; при 'at'.

на русском языке,
in [the] Russian language (loc. sing. of русский язык).

в трёх томах.
in three volumes (loc. pl. of три and том).

EXERCISES 3

New words. Write out and arrange as before. Key below.

английский	English	начало	beginning
власть	power	о	(with loc.) about
вся	all (variant of все, see 1.8.3)	перевод	translation
		план	plan
выпуск	issue	подготовил	prepared
вышли	went/have gone out	при	(with loc.) at
государственный	state (adj.)	приложение	supplement
день	day	резюме	summary
избранный	selected	русский	Russian
издается	is being/has been published	с	(with gen.) from, off
		сборник	symposium, collection of articles
к	(with dat.) to, up to		
книжный	book (adj.)	следующий	following
коллектив	collective	совет	soviet, council
летопись	chronicle, annals	составленный	compiled
литература	literature (not necessarily fiction)	статья	article
		три	three
на	(with loc.) on, in		

1.4. NOUN DECLENSION

Do not be put off by the apparently formidable table of variant endings that follows; study it carefully, using the notes as a guide to recognising the regularities as well as the aberrations.

The most important regularity is that all three genders have parallel 'hard' and 'soft' declensions which are basically alike but differ in the vowel sound of their endings. Thus, in the fem., пьеса, declined 'hard', has acc. and gen.

21

пьесу and пьесы, whereas неделя, declined 'soft', shows the endings неделю and недели. This correspondence of sounds can be followed throughout the declensions as an aid to learning.

Other notable similarities are those between the masculine and neuter declensions almost throughout, and in the dat., instr. and loc. plural, where the 'hard' and 'soft' ending sets -ам, -ами, -ах and -ям, -ями, -ях appear in all three genders.

With these likenesses in mind, attention can be paid to deviations such as the extra declension for feminine nouns ending in the soft sign -ь, the 'animate'/'inanimate' distinction in the acc. sing. masculine and the accusative plural, and the complete disappearance of endings in the feminine and neuter genitive plural.

	MASCULINE		FEMININE			NEUTER	
Sing.	'house'	'museum'	'play'	'week'	'speech'	'place'	'edition'
Nom.	дом	музей	пьеса	неделя	речь	место	издание
Acc.	[if animate noun, like nom., else like gen.]		пьесу	неделю	речь	место	издание
Gen.	дома	музея	пьесы	недели	речи	места	издания
Dat.	дому	музею	пьесе	неделе	речи	месту	изданию
Instr.	домом	музеем	пьесой	неделей	речью	местом	изданием
Loc.	доме	музее	пьесе	неделе	речи	месте	издании

Plural							
Nom.	домы	музеи	пьесы	недели	речи	места	издания
Acc.	[if animate noun, like genitive. If inanimate, like nominative]						
Gen.	домов	музеев	пьес	недель	речей	мест	изданий
Dat.	домам	музеям	пьесам	неделям	речям	местам	изданиям
Instr.	домами	музеями	пьесами	неделями	речями	местами	изданиями
Loc.	домах	музеях	пьесах	неделях	речях	местах	изданиях

Notes

1. In the accusative case, the masculine singular and all genders in the plural use the genitive form for nouns denoting living creatures. Otherwise the nominative form is used.

2. Neuter nouns ending in -ие and feminine nouns ending in -ия have the endings -и in the locative singular and -ий in the genitive plural; *eg* рецензия 'review' has the gen. pl. рецензий as in Летопись рецензий 'Chronicle of

reviews', and заглавие 'title, heading' has gen. pl. заглавий as in указатель заглавий 'index of titles'.

3. Many masculine nouns lose the last vowel of the stem in oblique (*ie* other than nominative) cases, *eg* день, gen. sing. дня, nom. pl. дни; конец, gen. sing. конца; список 'list', gen. sing. списка; рисунок 'drawing, figure' as in с рисунками 'with drawings' (с with instrumental = 'with'); иностранец 'foreigner' as in для иностранцев 'for foreigners' (для with genitive = 'for').

4. Where masculine nouns end in г, ж, к, х, ч, ш or щ, the nominative plural ending is -и not -ы, even though the declension is otherwise 'hard', *eg* вестник 'bulletin', nom. pl. вестники; итог 'result', nom. pl. итоги; очерк 'outline, sketch', nom. pl. очерки; стих 'verse', nom. pl. стихи 'poetry'; тираж 'size of edition', nom. pl. тиражи.

5. Likewise, where feminine nouns end in га, жа, ка, ха, ча, ша or ща, the genitive singular and nominative plural endings are -и, not -ы, although the declension is otherwise 'hard', *eg* книга 'book', gen. sing. and nom. pl. книги; библиотека/библиотеки 'library'; записка/записки 'note' (in pl. 'notes' or 'transactions').

EXERCISES 4

New words

библиотека	library	место	place
вестник	bulletin; messenger	очерк	outline, sketch
для	(with gen.) for	пьеса	play
дом	house	рецензия	review
заглавие	title, heading	речь	speech
записка	note; (in pl.: notes, transactions)	рисунок	drawing, figure
		список	list
издание	edition; impression; publication	стих	verse (in pl.: poetry)
		тираж	size of edition, no. of copies
иностранец	foreigner		
итог	result	указатель	index

Translate into English. (All words have been introduced previously in the course and case endings can be identified from the table above).

1. В школе.

2. Цена книги.

3. Автор рецензии.

4. Библиотека имени В. И. Ленина.
5. Очерк физики для иностранцев.
6. Библиография статей о войне 1941–45.
7. Введение к роману.

Key
1. In [the] school. (в: prep. with locative).
2. The price of the book. (книга in genitive).
3. The author of the review. (рецензия in genitive).
4. Library named after V. I. Lenin. (имени followed by gen.).
5. Outline of physics for foreigners. (gen. of физика).
6. Bibliography of articles about the war [of] 1941−45. (gen. pl. of статья, о followed by loc. sing. of война).
7. Introduction to the novel. (к followed by dat. sing. of роман).

1.5. ADJECTIVES AND ADVERBS

1.5.1. *Attributive adjectives.* Adjectives agree with the noun they qualify in number, gender and case, as in French, German and Latin. When used attributively (*eg* 'the *red* book'), they usually precede the noun, as in English. When used predicatively (*eg* 'the book is *red*'), they often appear in a shortened form (see 1.5.2).

Adjectives in the singular have one basic form for *each* gender. In the plural, there is one basic declension applying to *all* genders. The precise form of the ending varies according to the 'hard' or 'soft' pronunciation of the consonant before it, in a similar way to the noun declensions.

Sing.	*MASCULINE*	*FEMININE*	*NEUTER*
Nom.	нов*ый* 'new'	нов*ая*	нов*ое*
Acc.	like nom. or gen., as nouns	нов*ую*	нов*ое*
Gen.	нов*ого*	нов*ой*	нов*ого*
Dat.	нов*ому*	нов*ой*	нов*ому*
Instr.	нов*ым*	нов*ой*	нов*ым*
Loc.	нов*ом*	нов*ой*	нов*ом*

Plural	ALL GENDERS
Nom.	новые
Acc.	[like nom. or gen., as nouns]
Gen.	новых
Dat.	новым
Instr.	новыми
Loc.	новых

Notes

1. Masculine and neuter adjectives are declined identically in the singular, except in the nom./acc.

2. Adjectives which are stressed on the ending have the form -ой in the nominative masc. singular, but are otherwise declined as above. Examples: большой 'great', другой 'other(s)'.

3. The ending -ого (or -его) in the masc. and neuter genitive singular is pronounced *in these endings only* as -ово (or -ево).

EXERCISES 5
New adjectives

алфавитный	alphabetical	иностранный	foreign (cf.
библиографический	bibliographical		иностранец
будущий	future, next		foreigner)
важный	important	исторический	historical (cf.
великий	great		история
восточный	eastern (cf.		history)
	восток east)	коммунисти-	Communist
высший	higher	ческий	(adj.)
главный	main, chief (cf.	краткий	short
	глава chapter;	московский	Muscovite (cf.
	head)		Москва
детский	childrens' (cf.		Moscow)
	дети children)	музыкальный	musical (cf.
другой	other(s)		музыка
западный	western (cf.		music)
	запад west)	некоторый	some, certain

Translate into English:
1. Краткий очерк русской истории.
2. Некоторые важные издания.
3. 'Исторические записки'.
4. Алфавитный список библиографий для высших школ.
5. Детская литература.

Key
1. Short outline of Russian history. (gen. sing. forms of русская история).
2. Some important editions [*or* publications]. (nom. plural throughout).
3. 'Historical notes'. (title of an important irregular series).
4. Alphabetical list of bibliographies for higher schools [*ie*, universities].
(gen. pl. of библиография, and gen. pl. of высшая школа after preposition для).
5. Childrens' literature.

1.5.2. Predicative adjectives. Many Russian adjectives have a shortened form which is used (in the nominative only) where the verb 'to be' occurs or is implied in the type of construction 'the book *is red*'. Since in Russian the verb 'to be' is usually omitted in the present tense — or shown by a dash — the result is often a noun followed by the shortened form of the adjective.

	Long form		*Short form*
nom. masc. sing.	составленный	'compiled'	составлен
nom. fem. sing.	составленная		составлена
nom. neuter sing.	составленное		составлено
nom. plural	составленные		составлены

Compare (a) 1967 составленный выпуск 'the issue compiled [in] 1967'.
      (b) этот сборник составлен А. Н. Шанским 'this symposium is [*or* has been] compiled by A. N. Shanskii'. (note adjectival ending of Шанский, here in instr.).

EXERCISES 6

New adjectives

немецкий	German	рабочий	working, worker (declined as adj., *ie* 'working person')
общий	general, common		
отдельный	separate (cf. отдел section, department)	северный	northern (cf. север north)
		французский	French
последний	last, latest	центральный	central
предметный	subject (adj., cf. предмет subject)	южный	southern (cf. юг south)

26

New nouns

академия	academy	произведение	work, production
бюллетень	bulletin	содержание	contents
вопрос	question, matter	справочник	handbook, guide
город	town	СССР (= Союз	USSR (=Union
известия	(neut. pl.) news, 'transactions'	Советских Социалистиче-	of Soviet Socialist
комитет	committee	ских Республик)	Republics)
народ	people, nation	студент	student
писатель	writer	техника	technology
правда	truth		

Translate into English:

1. Русско–немецкий математический словарь.

2. Общие вопросы техники.

3. Центральный комитет Коммунистической партии Советского Союза (ЦК КПСС).

4. Французский рабочий класс и советский народ.

5. Бюллетень Института русского языка при Московском государственном университете (МГУ).

6. Предметный указатель к библиографии.

Key

1. Russian-German mathematical dictionary.

2. General questions of technology.

3. Central Committee of the Communist Party of the Soviet Union.

4. The French working class and the Soviet people.

5. Bulletin of the Institute of Russian Language at the Moscow State University. (при taking locative case).

6. Subject index to the bibliography. (к with dative).

1.5.3. Comparison of adjectives. The *comparative* form of an adjective (*eg* high*er*) is expressed in two ways:

(a) Used attributively, by adding более 'more' or менее 'less' before the basic adjective, *eg* более важное дело 'a more important matter'. A few attributive comparatives end in -ший and are declined like other adjectives.

Some of these also have a superlative meaning. They include:

высший	higher, highest	(высокий	high)
лучший	better, best	(хороший	good)
меньший	smaller	(маленький	small)
старший	older, eldest	(старый	old)

(b) Used predicatively, by giving the adjective the invariable ending -ee, *eg* мое дело важнее вашего, or мое дело важнее, чем ваше 'my business is more important than yours'.

The *superlative* of an adjective (high*est*) can be formed in two ways:

(a) Using самый before the adjective, agreeing with it in number, gender and case, *eg* самая редкая книга 'the rarest book'.

(b) Altering the ending of the adjective to -айший or -ейший, which is then declined in the usual way, *eg* новейшая книга 'the newest book'.

1.5.4. Adverbs. Many adverbs are derived from adjectives by a simple alteration in the ending (cf. English bad/bad*ly*). This is usually to -o, but for 'soft' adjectives to -e. *eg* ежегодный 'annual' (adj.), ежегодно 'annually'.

Adjectives ending in -ский yield adverbs ending in -ски, *eg* исторический 'historical', исторически 'historically'. A special usage is the prefixing of по- to an adverb in -ски to mean 'in the manner, or language, of . . .', *eg* по-английски 'in English', по-русски 'in Russian'.

EXERCISES 7
New words

более	more	маленький	small
ваш	your(s)	менее	less
включительно	inclusive(ly)	меньший	smaller
высокий	high	много	(indeclinable, with gen.) much, many
высший	higher, highest		
дело	affair, matter, business	несколько	(indeclinable, with gen.) several, a few, some
ежегодно	annually	особенно	especially
ежемесячно	monthly (adv.)	повторно	again
еженедельно	weekly (adv.)	ранний	early
естественный	natural	самый	most; the very . . .; same
лучший	better, best	старый	old

28

старший	older, eldest		только	only
страница	page		уже	already
так	so, thus		хороший	good
также	also, as well		чем	than
тоже	also, as well			

Translate into English:

1. Несколько томов нового издания А. П. Чехова — уже в Научном библиотеке университета.

2. Северо-восточная Азия в современной советской литературе: рекомендательная библиография.

3. Редкие книги немецких издательств: аннотированный каталог.

4. Указатель заглавий — на стр.[анах] 432–448 вкл.[ючительно].

5. Книга сост.[авлена] А. С. Волконским и др. [угими].

Key

1. Several volumes of the new edition of A. P. Chekhov [are] already in the Scientific [*or* Research] Library of the university. (несколько is invariable and followed by gen.).

2. North-Eastern Asia in contemporary Soviet literature: a recommendatory bibliography.

3. Rare books of [*or* from] German publishers: an annotated catalogue.

4. An index of titles [is] on pages 432–448 inclusive.

5. The book [is *or* has been] compiled by A. S. Volkonskii and others.

1.6. PERSONAL NAMES

Russian personal names have traditionally had three components — forename (имя); patronymic (отчество, derived from the father's forename); and surname (фамилия). This three-part name has now become standard in the Soviet Union, even for nationalities among whom it was not previously customary. Examples:

Лев Николаевич Толстой   Владимир Ильич Ульянов (Ленин).

Анна Андреевна Ахматова   Ибрагим Абдуллаевич Азизбеков.

Сергей Натанович Бернштейн   Ольга Васильевна Лепешинская

With certain exceptions (perhaps the most frequently-met being surnames of Ukrainian origin ending in -енко, which are indeclinable, such as Шевченко, Кириленко), all parts of the personal name are declined, either as nouns, as

29

adjectives (in surnames with adjectival endings like Толстой or Шанский), or (in surnames with the common endings -ов, -ев and -ин) in a 'mixed' part-noun, part-adjective declension:

	MASCULINE		FEMININE	
Nom.	Козлов,	Пушкин	Козлова,	Пушкина
Acc.	Козлова,	Пушкина	Козлову,	Пушкину
Gen.	Козлова,	Пушкина	Козлов*ой*,	Пушкин*ой*
Dat.	Козлову,	Пушкину	Козлов*ой*,	Пушкин*ой*
Instr.	Козлов*ым*,	Пушкин*ым*	Козлов*ой*,	Пушкин*ой*
Loc.	Козлове,	Пушкине	Козлов*ой*,	Пушкин*ой*

PLURAL

Nom.	Козловы,	Пушкины
Acc.	Козлов*ых*,	Пушкин*ых*
Gen.	Козлов*ых*,	Пушкин*ых*
Dat.	Козлов*ым*,	Пушкин*ым*
Instr.	Козлов*ыми*,	Пушкин*ыми*
Loc.	Козлов*ых*,	Пушкин*ых*

Adjectival forms of ending are in *italics*. Notice that the accusative form in the plural and masc. singular is always the same as the genitive, since surnames will always, of course, refer to 'animate objects'!

1.7. NUMERALS

1.7.1. Cardinal and ordinal numerals

	Cardinal numerals ('one', etc.)	Ordinal numerals ('first', etc.)
1	один, одна, одно	первый
2	два, две	второй
3	три	третий
4	четыре	четвёртый
5	пять	пятый
6	шесть	шестой
7	семь	седьмой
8	восемь	восьмой
9	девять	девятый
10	десять	десятый

	Cardinal numerals ('one', etc.)	Ordinal numerals ('first', etc.)
11	одиннадцать	одиннадцатый
12	двенадцать	двенадцатый
13	тринадцать	тринадцатый
14	четырнадцать	четырнадцатый
15	пятнадцать	пятнадцатый
16	шестнадцать	шестнадцатый
17	семнадцать	семнадцатый
18	восемнадцать	восемнадцатый
19	девятнадцать	девятнадцатый
20	двадцать	двадцатый
21	двадцать один	двадцать первый
22	двадцать два	двадцать второй
30	тридцать	тридцатый
40	сорок	сороковой
50	пятьдесят	пятидесятый
60	шестьдесят	шестидесятый
70	семьдесят	семидесятый
80	восемьдесят	восьмидесятый
90	девяносто	девяностый
100	сто	сотый
200	двести	двухсотый
300	триста	трёхсотый
400	четыреста	четырёхсотый
500	пятьсот	пятисотый
600	шестьсот	шестисотый
700	семьсот	семисотый
800	восемьсот	восьмисотый
900	девятьсот	девятисотый
1000	тысяча	тысячный
2000	две тысячи	двухтысячный
5000	пять тысяч	пятитысячный

'one-half': половина, 'one-third': треть, 'one-quarter': четверть. 'the year nineteen sixty-eight': тысяча девятьсот шестьдесят восьмой год, 1968 г.

1.7.2. Declension of numerals. All numerals vary their form according to their grammatical function, like nouns and adjectives. Declension of cardinals in most cases closely resembles one or other of the noun declensions, and oblique forms are usually quite recognisable, with the following possible exceptions:

	2	3	4
Nom.	два, две	три	четыре
Acc.		[like nom. or gen.]	
Gen.	двух	трёх	четырёх
Dat.	двум	трём	четырём
Instr.	двумя	тремя	четырьмя
Loc.	двух	трёх	четырёх

1.7.3. Case forms following numerals. Except where they appear in the nominative, numerals agree in case with the nouns and adjectives to which they apply, *eg* в трёх отдельных томах 'in three separate volumes' (locative case following в),

BUT . . .

(a) два, три, четыре in the *nominative* case are followed by nouns *in the genitive singular* and *adjectives in the genitive plural, eg* три других вопроса 'three other questions'.

(b) Numerals from пять onwards in the *nominative* case are followed by *nouns and adjectives in the genitive plural, eg* шесть древних городов 'six ancient towns'.

EXERCISES 8

New words associated with numerals

до н.э. [нашей эры]	в.с. ('up to our era')	номер, №	number; issue
копейка	kopek (1/100 of a rouble)	н.э. [нашей эры]	A.D. ('of our era')
лета	(gen. pl. лет) years. (cf. год which also = year. The distinction is not explained here, since it chiefly affects translation *into* Russian)	рубль	rouble
		середина	middle
		серия	series
		сессия	session
		созыв	convocation
		столетие	century (cf. век, also = century)
		съезд	congress

32

фунт	pound (£)	часть	part
цифра	figure	экземпляр	copy, specimen

Translate into English:

1. Екатерина Вторая.

2. Ф. М. Достоевский: избранные произведения в восьми томах.

3. Известия Академии Наук СССР [АН СССР]. Серия история, выпуск третий [вып. 3-ий].

4. Рабочий класс в Донбассе в тридцатых годах.

5. Роман в первом половине девятнадцатого века.

6. Цена — два фунта, т.е. [то есть, i.е.] четыре рубля двадцать восемь копеек.

7. Тираж десять тысяч экземляров [экз.].

8. Верховный (=supreme) Совет СССР: третья сессия четвёртого созыва.

Key

1. Catherine the Second (the Great, 1729–96).

2. F. M. Dostoevskii: selected works in eight volumes.

3. News (*or* Transactions) of the Academy of Sciences of the USSR. Series 'History', third issue. (Inversion of phrases with ordinal numbers, like the last two words, is common).

4. The working class in the Donbas (Donets Basin) in the thirtieth years (*ie* the Thirties).

5. The novel in the first half of the nineteenth century.

6. The price [is] two pounds, *ie* four roubles twenty-eight kopeks. (Note that рубль is masc., and рубля is thus a 'soft' masc. gen. *sing.* ending after четыре. копеек is genitive *plural* after '28').

7. Size of edition [*or* impression] ten thousand copies.

8. Supreme Soviet of the USSR: third session of the fourth convocation.

1.8. PRONOUNS

1.8.1. *Personal pronouns ('I', 'you', etc.)*

Nom. я (I); ты(you); он, оно(he,it); она (she); мы (we); вы(you); они (they).

Acc.	меня	тебя	его	её	нас	вас	их
Gen.	меня	тебя	его	её	нас	вас	их
Dat.	мне	тебе	ему	ей	нам	вам	им
Instr.	мной	тобой	им	ею	нами	вами	ими
Loc.	мне	тебе	нём	ней	нас	вас	них

33

Notes

1. Where preceded by a preposition, он, она, оно, они are prefixed by н-, *eg* у него, для них, с ним, о нём.

2. его is pronounced as ево, as in the adjectival ending.

1.8.2. *Possessive pronouns ('my', 'your', etc.)*

мой, моя, моё, мои	my	
твой, твоя, твоё, твои	your	
свой, своя, своё, свои	one's own	fully declined like adjectives
наш, наша, наше, наши	our	
ваш, ваша, ваше, ваши	your	
его	his, its	not declined, being the
её	her, its	genitive forms of the personal
их	their	pronouns in 1.8.1.

1.8.3. *Other pronouns.* The most important of these are кто 'who', что 'what' and весь 'all'.

Nom.	кто 'who'	что 'what' (pronounced што)
Acc.	кого	что
Gen.	кого	чего
Dat.	кому	чему
Instr.	кем	чем
Loc.	ком	чём

весь is declined in all three genders in the singular:

	MASCULINE	FEMININE	NEUTER	PLURAL
Nom.	весь	вся	всё	все
Acc.	весь, всего	всю	всё	все, всех
Gen.	всего	всей	всего	всех
Dat.	всему	всей	всему	всем
Instr.	всем	всей	всем	всеми
Loc.	всём	всей	всём	всех

1.9. PREPOSITIONS

Prepositions (*eg* English 'to', 'by', 'for') in Russian oblige the use of various cases for the nouns, adjectives and pronouns which they govern, *eg*

кроме этого	'besides this'	(кроме governs the genitive)
к этому	'towards this'	(к governs the dative).

Some prepositions govern more than one case, with differing meanings, *eg*
в библиотеке   '*in* the library' (в governing the locative), BUT
в библиотеку   '*into* the library' (в governing the accusative).
Several prepositions alter their form where this is felt necessary for easier
pronunciation:

в may appear as во

к „   „   „ ко

с „   „   „ со

о „   „   „ об, обо

List of prepositions. The most common Russian prepositions are listed below,
arranged by the case which they govern. A number have already been
introduced.

Prepositions governing the accusative

в, во	into	про	about, concerning
за	for (for alternative translations consult dictionary)	с, со	about, approximately
		через	over, across, through
на	on to, on (many other meanings in set phrases)		
по	up to (many other meanings in set phrases)		

Prepositions governing the genitive

без	without	от	from, away from
вместо	instead of	после	after
для	for	против	against
до	up to, until, as far as	с, со	from, down from
из	out of, from	среди	among
кроме	besides	у	at, near, by, in the possession of

Prepositions governing the dative

к, ко	towards	по	according to, along

Prepositions governing the instrumental

за	behind, after; for (and other meanings in set phrases)	над	over, above
		под	under
		с, со	with
между	between		

Prepositions governing the locative

в, во	in	по	after
на	on (and other meanings in set phrases)	при	with, in the presence (*or* time) of
о, об, обо	about, on		

EXERCISES 9

New words

всесоюзный	all-Union	союз	union
международный	international	то есть, т.е.	that is, *ie*
отечественный	patriotic	тот, та, то, те	that
послесловие	postscript, after-word	эпоха	epoch, age
рукопись	manuscript	этот, эта, это, эти	this

Translate into English:

1. Без цены, б.ц.
2. До наших дней.
3. История города за сорок лет.
4. Из моих произведениях.
5. К вопросу о роле (Guess! Nom. is роль) интеллигенции (Guess!) во Великой Октябрьской`(Guess!) социалистической революции.
6. Между двумя войнами.
7. План выпуска литературы на 1972 год.
8. Газета на английском языке.
9. От 5-ого до 2-ого столетий до н.э.
10. По Великой Отечественной Войне.
11. Под редакцией проф. А. П. Боборыкина.
12. При Петре Первом.
13. Речь против империализма Америки.
14. Ленин с нами!
15. Ленин среди нас!
16. У ней собрание редких рукописей.

Key

1. Without price (unpriced).
2. Up to our [own] days.
3. A [*or* the] history of the [*or* a] town for [*or* over] forty years.

4. From my works.

5. Towards [*or* on] the question of [*or* about] the role of the intelligent-sia in the Great October Socialist Revolution. (This is the full Soviet title of the October Revolution of 1917: 7th November by the modern calendar.)

6. Between two wars.

7. Plan of issue of literature [*ie* forthcoming publications] for the year 1972. (Special usage of на with accusative).

8. A newspaper in the English language. (Special usage of на with locative).

9. From the 5th to the 2nd century B.C. (gen. pl. of столетие).

10. After the Great Patriotic War. (по with locative. The title is the usual Soviet name for the Second World War, or more strictly the war in which the USSR was involved after the German invasion of 22nd June 1941.)

11. Under the editorship of Prof. A. P. Boborykin.

12. In the time of Peter the First (the Great, 1672–1725).

13. A speech against the imperialism of America.

14. Lenin is with us!

15. Lenin is among us!

16. She has (*literally* at her [is]) a collection of rare manuscripts. (This construction with у is a common way of expressing possession where English usually uses 'to have'.)

1.10. VERBS

1.10.1. Infinitive form. Usually rendered in English as '*to* do', '*to* see', etc. This is the form in which Russian verbs are entered in dictionaries, and is usually recognisable by the ending -ть, *eg* читать 'to read', писать 'to write'. A few infinitives end in -ти, *eg* идти 'to go'.

1.10.2. Present tense. Most verbs are conjugated with the following pattern of endings:

1st person singular	(I)		-ю or -у
2nd „ „	(you)		-шь
3rd „ „	(he, she, it)		-т
1st „ plural	(we)		-м
2nd „ „	(you)		-те
3rd „ „	(they)		-ют or -ут; -ят or -ат

Examples:

читать to read	выйти to go out, be published
я читаю	я выйду
ты читаешь	ты выйдёшь
он, она, оно читает	он, она, оно выдёт
мы читаем	мы выйдём
вы читаете	вы выйдёте
они читают	они выйдут

Certain verbs undergo consonant changes in some forms of the present tense, *eg* in писать 'to write': пишу, пишешь, пишет, etc.

1.10.3. Past tense. Russian verbs form their past tense very simply, replacing the -ть ending of the infinitive by the ending -л (masc. sing.), -ла (fem. sing.), -ло (neut. sing.) and -ли (plural), according to the gender and number of their subject, *eg*

Masculine: Подготовил к печати Н. И. Смирнов (from подготовить 'to prepare', *ie* 'N. I. Smirnov prepared [the work] for [*literally* towards] the press').

Feminine: Хрестоматию составила Л. Н. Платонова (from составить 'to compile', *ie* 'L. N. Platonova compiled the collection of readings').

Plural: Журнали выходили ежемесячно (from выходить 'to go out, appear, be published', *ie* 'The journals appeared monthly').

1.10.4. Reflexive verbs. These are usually verbs of which the subject and object refer to the same thing (*eg* English 'to wash oneself', French 'se laver', German 'sich waschen'. In Russian they assume exactly the same grammatical endings as other verbs, but with the added suffix -ся (-сь after vowels). However, the meaning is not always reflexive. It may be passive, *eg*

он кончает статью	'he is finishing the article'
статья кончается	'the article is being finished'
статья кончалась	'the article was being finished'

Other examples are публикуются впервые 'are being published for the first time' (публиковать = 'to publish', hence публиковаться = 'to *be* published'); and готовятся к выпуску 'are being prepared for issue' (готовить = 'to prepare', hence готовиться = 'to *be* prepared').

1.10.5. Aspects and the future tense. Most Russian verbs are used in pairs of basic forms, usually similar in appearance. One of these forms, or *aspects*, is normally used to indicate a completed action (the *perfective aspect*), the other to denote an action still in progress (the *imperfective aspect*)

Examples: читать (ipfve) 'to read, be reading'
прочитать (pfve) 'to read, to have read'
я читал газету 'I was reading the newspaper'
я прочитал газету 'I finished reading the newspaper, read it right through'

Further examples of perfective/imperfective verb pairs:

писать (ipfve) ⎫
написать (pfve) ⎬ 'to write'

получать (ipfve) ⎫
получить (pfve) ⎬ 'to receive'

выходить (ipfve) ⎫ 'to go out, be published'
выйти (pfve) ⎬ (unrelated basic forms)

Naturally, a perfective verb cannot be used to express a 'present' meaning, and in fact these verbs when used in their 'present' tense forms have a 'future' meaning:

я прочитаю газету 'I shall read the newspaper'
серия выйдёт в декабре 'the series will be published in December'

Imperfective verbs may be given a 'future' meaning by using the future tense of быть ('to be'): буду, будешь, etc.: он будет писать еженедельно 'he will be writing every week'.

1.10.6. Participles (verbal adjectives). Two varieties of these adjectives derived from verbs need introduction, the *present participle active* and *past participle passive* (*eg* English 'collect*ing*' and 'collect*ed*' respectively, from 'to collect'). The participles in Russian are declined like other adjectives.

The present participle active is characterised by the adjectival ending -щий, -щая, -щее, etc., *eg* читающий 'reading', from читать, cf. читают 'they read'. Present participles active can also be formed from reflexive verbs, in which case they retain the -ся suffix *after* the ending, which gives them an unfamiliar appearance: продолжающиеся издания 'continuing publications' (from продолжаться to be continued); развивающиеся страны 'developing countries' (from развиваться 'to develop', literally 'to draw oneself out').

39

The past participle passive is marked by the adjectival endings -нный, -нная, etc. (which are the more frequent) and -тый, -тая, etc. Both sets of endings appear in their short forms when used predicatively:

следующие книги изданы не бу́дут 'the following books will not be published' (изданы is the 'short' nom. plural form of the past participle passive изданный, from издать 'to publish'. Note also the present participle active следующий, from следовать 'to follow').

книга составлена коллективом 'the book [is *or* was] compiled by a collective' (составлена is the 'short' nom. sing. fem. form of составленный from составлять 'to compile').

2. TRANSLITERATION

Transliteration is, strictly speaking, the use of one alphabet to represent the characters of another. Less strictly, the term is often used as a synonym for 'transcription', to mean the indication of the *sounds* of a language by characters of an alphabet in which it is not customarily written. Since the Roman alphabet normally uses no more than 26 basic characters, and the Cyrillic now used for Russian has 32 characters, the supply of Roman letters has to be eked out with diacritic marks, combinations of letters or both, in order to achieve an approach to the accurate pronunciation of the Cyrillic original, or a re-transliteration back to Cyrillic.

Another source of confusion is that many of the sounds of Russian which need to be rendered demand varying spellings in the Roman alphabet to make them recognisable and 'pronounceable' in different West European languages. The 'popular' transliterations used, for instance, in newspapers and other non-specialist works, need to put readability before an unambiguous recording of the Cyrillic original. Hence the frequent appearance of the poet Евтушенко as 'Yevtushenko' and 'Jewtuschenko' in many English and German publications respectively, as a potential source of error in filing or in checking an alphabetical list; or French 'Lénine' and English 'Trotsky' to reproduce Ленин and Троцкий. Nor is it uncommon for authors of Russian origin, who have written in Russian, to adopt a simplified or (for example) Anglicised form of name when writing in English: the historian George Vernadsky, for instance, now writing in English, used a form of name in Russian which could be transliterated Georgii [Vladimirovich] Vernadskii.

2.1. TRANSLITERATION FROM CYRILLIC TO ROMAN
Of the many transliteration 'systems' intended to meet the specialist's requirements for accuracy and consistency, the three most often met with in English-speaking countries are:

1. The 'British' system of British Standard BS 2979:1958, which observes English spelling conventions and is therefore difficult for non-English speakers

41

to follow. It is commonly used (though often with its few diacritics omitted) in catalogues and bibliographies in the UK, and with slight (and different) variations at the British Museum and the Bodleian Library.

2. *The Library of Congress system,* which also follows English spelling conventions, differs from the British Standard system in its rendering of 6 Cyrillic characters, only 3 of which affect filing order. It is the most widespread system in English-speaking America, and is employed, of course, in all LC publications, but *not* by the New York Public Library, which uses its own system in the published catalogue of its extremely rich Slavonic Collection (on which see 4.2.4).

3. *The International Organisation for Standards ISO/R9 system,* patterned on the spelling of certain Slavonic languages which do use the Roman alphabet, such as Czech and Croat. It shows a preference for diacritics in contrast to the multi-letter combinations favoured by 1 and 2, and differs from the British Standard system in its rendering of 13 Cyrillic characters, 9 of which affect filing order.

The table below takes the 'British' system of BS 2979:1958 as a yardstick, and shows the differences between it and the LC system, ISO/R9, the NYPL, BM and Bodleian systems, and 'popular' French and German variations.

Cyrillic	BS 2979:1958	Variations
а	a	
б	b	
в	v	German often: w
г	g	French sometimes: gu
д	d	
е	e	NYPL: ye at beginning of word or syllable
ё	ë	NYPL usually: io. Diaresis often omitted
ж	zh	ISO: ž. French often: j. German often: sh
з	z	German often: s
и	i	
й	ï	ISO: j. In BM, final -ий = y, final -ый = uy
к	k	
л	l	
м	m	
н	n	

Cyrillic	BS 2979:1958	Variations
о	o	
п	p	
р	r	
с	s	
т	t	
у	u	French often: ou
ф	f	
х	kh	ISO: h. German and elsewhere often: ch. Sometimes, misleadingly: x
ц	ts	ISO: c. NYPL: tz. German often: z
ч	ch	ISO: č. German often: tsch. French often: tch
ш	sh	ISO: š. German often: sch. French often: ch
щ	shch	ISO: šč. German often: schtsch. French often: chtch
ъ	"	Omitted in BS and most other systems at end of word
ы	ȳ	BM: ui. Bodleian: î. Most systems omit bar
ь	'	Often omitted
э	é	ISO, LC, NYPL: ė
ю	yu	ISO, German: ju. LC: i͡u. French often: iou
я	ya	ISO, German: ja. LC: i͡a. French often: ia

(Obsolete characters)

i	i	
ѣ	ê	ISO, NYPL: ě. LC: i͡e
ѳ	ḟ	Some systems omit dot
ѵ	y̆	ISO, LC, NYPL: ẏ. BM, Bodleian: i

2.2. TRANSLITERATION FROM ROMAN TO CYRILLIC

Russian conventions in transliterating *from* Roman *into* Cyrillic can on occasion cause problems in recognition when English or other non-Russian words appear in a Russian text. In most cases, careful pronunciation as if the word were Russian, and a little imagination, will give the clue, but points to bear in mind in transliteration from English are:

English a is often rendered by Cyrillic э

„	h	„	„	„	„	г, sometimes х
„	j	„	„	„	„	дж
„	l	„	„	„	„	ль, ie a 'soft' л. (Russian л alone is pronounced much further back in the throat than in Southern English, closer to the Scottish pronunciation.)
„	unvoiced th	„	„	„		т
„	voiced th	„	„	„		з
„	w		„	„	„	у or в

Thus three English literary figures appear as Вильям Шекспир, Томас Гарди and Джордж Бернард Шо. The western principality becomes Уэльс, and a well-known statesman is transformed into Эдуард Хит (or, less happily, Гит).

In transliteration of French, the many unpronounced letters are omitted, giving, for example, Жан-Жак Руссо. Difficulties with German umlauted vowels result in Йоханн Вольфганг фон Гёте (Goethe) and Мюнхен (München).

3. NOTES ON CATALOGUING

The cataloguing of material in Russian presents certain special problems arising from the language, the Cyrillic alphabet, the conditions under which Soviet works are written and published, and Soviet conventions in book production. Some of the more commonly-occurring difficulties are considered here. 'AACR' references are to rule numbers in the *Anglo-American cataloguing rules. British text* of 1967.

3.1. LANGUAGE AND TRANSLITERATION

Unless a separate Cyrillic file is maintained in the order of the Cyrillic alphabet, catalogue entries for works in Russian will require at least a transliterated heading for filing purposes (cf. AACR 44B, especially 44B1e, exception, recommending systematic rather than traditional transliteration). Whether the body of the entry is given in Cyrillic or transliterated – Romanized, in the AACR terminology – will depend on the importance attached to preservation of the original, availability and cost of Cyrillic typing or printing facilities, and any limitations imposed by machine-readable catalogue records.

3.2. HEADINGS

3.2.1. Full personal names. The full personal name of an author, including forename and patronymic (see 1.6), is usually stated only in the colophon, which now normally appears on the last printed page of books published in the Soviet Union. Even here, the full name is only given for the author or authors directly responsible for writing the book. Editors, and contributors to collective works, are usually given initials only. Current Soviet bibliographies rarely show more than initials, or forename only.

3.2.2. Grammatical form of name. Personal names requiring inclusion in the catalogue entry may appear in a variety of grammatical forms which need to

be recognised and sometimes converted to follow cataloguing conventions. Note particularly that:
- the *genitive* case will appear after под ред. ('under the editorship of . . .') and similar phrases.
- the *dative* case will appear in formulae of presentation in Festschriften and the like, *eg* П. А. Павлову к 75-летию со дня рождения ('*to* P. A. Pavlov on the occasion of his 75th birthday').
- the *instrumental* case will appear after past participles such as сост.[авлен] И. А. Козловой ('compiled *by* I. A. Kozlova').

All personal names in headings are converted to the *nominative* case. For declensions, see 1.6, and for a quick-recognition table see the introduction to the vocabulary (section 7.1).

3.2.3. Names of non-Russian origin. Authors of non-Russian origin writing in Russian may appear in headings under the 'native' form of their name, or in a transliteration of the Russian rendering of that native form, *eg* Herzen *or* Gertsen (from Герцен), Baudouin de Courtenay *or* Boduén de Kurtené (from Бодуэн де Куртенэ). AACR gives no direct guidance on this. Decisions in individual cases will depend partly on treatment of the name in reference sources, where it may have become regarded as Russianised (*eg* Kyukhel'beker, from Кюхельбекер, rather than Küchelbecker), and partly on the frequency of the author's writings, if any, in the language of his 'native' name.

3.2.4. Authors and editors. Many Soviet publications are written by a number of authors in collaboration, and/or edited by a group acting as a редакционная коллегия ('editorial board'). Where this occurs, the correct catalogue heading to be allotted under Western conventions may be in doubt, and there is a danger of the entry's receiving a heading untraceable in Soviet bibliographies. The degree of responsibility for a work exercised by an editor (редактор), or even a 'responsible editor' (ответственный редактор) or 'chief editor' (главный редактор) varies greatly, and this, together with the number of 'editors' of various kinds often involved with a single work, may result in a variety of interpretations of the relevant cataloguing rules (cf. AACR 4, 5A), and hence of headings allotted. The Soviet practice of preferring the title as heading in the absence of an identifiable *author* may often be found useful. The colophon will act as a guide in this (see also 3.5).

3.2.5. Institutional responsibility. It is common practice for Soviet scholarly and educational works to carry at the head of their title-page the name of the institution under whose auspices the book has been produced, or the name of the ministry or department which has approved its use for, say, teaching purposes. The mention of this institution on a title-page does not, however, in many cases, imply that it has the degree of responsibility for a work's appearance which would justify an entry in the catalogue (cf. AACR 4, f/n 6 and 33G). Where a single author can be identified, his name is almost certainly to be preferred as a heading. Even in a case of collective authorship, entry under editor and/or title is generally more useful (cf. 3.2.4), and exceptions are usually fairly obvious, notably reports, proceedings, statutes, regulations, etc., produced by government and Party organisations and other bodies in pursuit of their official functions.

Standard Soviet bibliographical practice is to regard an institution's name thus quoted in the same way as a series note (whether or not it includes the name of, and number in, a series), and to state it in round brackets in the bibliographical description (see 4.1.1).

3.3. IMPRINT

3.3.1. Place. Note the standard Russian bibliographical abbreviations for towns most frequently occurring as places of publication:

Л.	Ленинград	(1924–)
М.	Москва	
П., Пг.	Петроград	(1914–24)
Спб.	Санктпетербургъ	(to 1914)

3.3.2. Publisher. Soviet publishing houses are often quoted in bibliographies and catalogue entries as an acronym or a set of initials: see the select list in 7.2.9 of present publishing houses. Certain others are listed in the complete vocabulary (7.3).

3.4. COLLATION: VOLUME STATEMENT

The number of volumes in a multi-volume set is often stated in the form of a sub-title, *eg* в трех томах ('in three volumes'). Inclusion of this statement in a catalogue entry can be useful both as a differentiation between editions and as an indication of progress in publishing an uncompleted set.

3.5. COLOPHONS

A colophon, or 'publishing particulars', is obliged by law to be printed in every Soviet publication except certain works intended for export. It normally appears on the last printed page, or, if not, on the back of the title-page. It contains, in a slightly varying order, information required for cataloguing purposes (author's full name, title, edition statement, publisher, etc.), and also data on the printing and publishing process for the work concerned, including dates when sent to compositor and when passed for printing; size of edition (тираж); censorship serial number; and price (also usually shown in the top left-hand corner of the outside back cover). Soviet publications in languages other than Russian usually contain a Russian-language colophon.

3.6. SERIALS

Many Soviet institutions publish regular or irregular serials of the 'proceedings' or 'transactions' type, characterised by such titles as бюллетень, ведомости, вестник, доклады, записки, известия, сборник, сообщения or труды. Identification and recording of these publications is often difficult: an institution may produce several such serials, each title sometimes being itself no more than a series title comprising several subject sections, which may split, re-form and divide again on a different pattern; numbering may be inconsistent or, particularly for early volumes, non-existent; and finally, the definition of some of them as serials at all may be open to doubt where the publishing institution's intentions are unclear (cf. AACR definition, p. 268). Headings for such serials are likely to be subject to AACR 6B, 'Entry under name of corporate body'. Guidance can be sought from the catalogues and bibliographies listed in 4.1.4 and 4.2.4 to 4.2.8.

4. BIBLIOGRAPHIES AND REFERENCE WORKS

This chapter gives an introduction to:
    4.1. Current bibliographies of Soviet publications.
    4.2. Retrospective bibliographies and catalogues useful for the identification of works in Russian.
    4.3. Quick-reference works in English giving information on Russia and the USSR.
    4.4. Russian-English dictionaries, general and specialised.

4.1. CURRENT BIBLIOGRAPHIES

Excellent current bibliographical coverage is now provided for most kinds of Soviet publication. The weekly all-Union bibliography of books (Книжная летопись), its annual cumulation (Ежегодник книги) and the weekly list of forthcoming books (Новые книги СССР) are described below in some detail, and all-Union bibliographies for other categories of publication more briefly. In all these bibliographies, entries are in Russian throughout, where necessary in a translation of the original with a note of the language of publication.

4.1.1. Книжная летопись (Knizhnaya letopis': 'Book chronicle'). This bibliography of books published in the Soviet Union appears in two 'issues' (выпуски). The *basic issue* (основной выпуск) appears weekly and contains material intended for a relatively wide readership, most of it available through the book trade: popular and scholarly monographs and pamphlets, handbooks, guides, textbooks, fiction, dictionaries, encyclopedias, atlases and irregular academic series of the 'труды' (proceedings) type.

    The *supplementary issue* (дополнительный выпуск), which appears monthly, is a selective listing of works expected to be of interest to a more limited range of readers, such as official publications, specialised instructional and technical material, books for the blind and thesis summaries (авторефераты).

    Both issues have included since 1934 material published in all languages anywhere in the USSR. They *exclude* 'ephemera'; works 'intended for a very limited readership'; and publications of less than 4 pages or produced in under 100 copies.

Arrangement of each weekly or monthly number is into 31 main subject classes. From no. 8 (1972) of the basic issue, the 31 classes appear in a re-organised form, which is shown as follows on the contents page:

Основные разделы:
1 Марксизм-ленинизм . . . .
2 Общественные науки в целом . . . .
3 Философские науки. Социология. Психология . . . . .
4 Экономика. Экономические науки . . . .
5 История. Исторические науки . . . .
6 Международное коммунистическое движение. Коммунистические и рабочие партии . . . .
7 Международные отношения. Внешняя и внутренняя политика государств . . . .
8 Международное профсоюзное движение . . . . . .
9 Международное движение молодежи . . . . . .
10 Государство и право. Юридические науки . . . . .
11 Военная наука. Военное дело . . . .
12 Статистика. Демография . . . .
13 Наука. Науковедение . . . .
14 Кибернетика. Семиотика. Информатика . . . . . .
15 Естественные науки . . . .
16 Техника. Промышленность . . . .
17 Сельское и лесное хозяйство. Сельскохозяйственные и лесохозяйственные науки . . . .
18 Транспорт . . . .
19 Связь . . . .
20 Заготовки. Торговля. Общественное питание . . . .
21 Коммунальное хозяйство. Бытовое обслуживание населения . .
22 Здравоохранение. Медицинские науки . . . . . .
23 Физическая культура. Спорт . . . .
24 Культура. Образование . . . .
25 Филологические науки . . . .
26 Художественная литература. Фольклор . . . . . .
27 Литература для детей. Фольклор для детей . . . . .
28 Искусство. Искусствоведение . . . .
29 Религия. Атеизм . . . .
30 Печать. Книговедение . . . .
31 Справочники общего характера. Энциклопедии. Календари. Сборники смешанного содержания . . . .

Fig. 1

English equivalents are:

1. Marxism-Leninism. 2. The social sciences in general. 3. Philosophical sciences. Sociology. Psychology. 4. Economics. Economic sciences. 5. History. Historical sciences. 6. The international communist movement.

Communist and workers' parties. 7. International relations. External and internal policy of states. 8. The international trade union movement. 9. The international youth movement. 10. The state and law. Legal sciences. 11. Military science. Military affairs. 12. Statistics. Demography. 13. Science. The study of science. 14. Cybernetics. Semiotics. Informatics. 15. Natural sciences. 16. Technology. Industry. 17. Agriculture and forestry. Agricultural and forest sciences. 18. Transport. 19. Communications. 20. Supply. Trade. Catering. 21. Local economy. Domestic services. 22. Health. Medical sciences. 23. Physical culture. Sport. 24. Culture. Education. 25. Literary and linguistic sciences. 26. Literature. Folklore. 27. Literature for children. Folklore for children. 28. Art. The study of art. 29. Religion. Atheism. 30. The press. The study of books. 31. Handbooks of a general nature. Encyclopedias. Calendars. Symposia with varied contents.

Layout of entries. Each main entry contains as many of the following elements as necessary:

1. Running item number within a yearly sequence.
2. Author (usually only surname and initials).
3. Title and subtitle, with supplied notes in square brackets.
4. Place of publication.
5. Publisher.
6. Date of publication.
7. Pagination and illustrations.
8. Series note and/or institution under whose auspices published, in round brackets. (see 3.2.5.)
9. Note of any bibliographies included.
10. Language, if other than Russian.
11. Height in centimetres.
12. Number of copies printed.
13. Price in roubles and kopeks.
14. Note on binding, if other than paper.
15. Whether first impression (п).
16. Classification.

Single volumes of a series or multi-volume set are when necessary given an individual description following that of the series or set as a whole.

Examples:

43797. **Смирнова Г. Е.** Основные направления современной буржуаз-
ной философии. Лекция по курсу философии.   [Л.], 1970. 16 с. (М-во
высш. и сред. спец. образования РСФСР. Ленингр. политехн. ин-т им.
М. И. Калинина). — Библиогр.: с. 15—16. — 21 см. 1.000 экз. 10 к. —
[70-66412] п   1(104)(075.8) + [016.3]

43798. **Мкрян М. М.** Мовсэс Хоренаци.   Ереван, «Айастан», 1970.
230 с. — На арм. яз. — 21 см. 5.000 экз. 66 к. В пер. — [70-28994] п
                                               90(479.25)(092)Хоренаци

43803. **Германская** история в новое и новейшее время. В 2-х т. Ред.
коллегия: С. Д. Сказкин [и др.]   М., «Наука», 1970. (АН СССР. Ин-т
всеобщей истории). — 22 см.
      Т. 1. [Авт. М. М. Смирин, С. Д. Сказкин и Л И. Гинцберг].   510 с.
с илл.; 3 л. илл. и карт. — 4.500 экз. 2 р. 15 к. В пер. — [70-64034] п
                                                          9(430)

43811. **Из истории** Татарии. [Сборник статей].   Казань, 1970. (М-во
просвещения РСФСР. Казан. гос. пед. ин-т. Учен. записки...) — 22 см.
      Сб. 4. [Ред. коллегия: ...Н. М. Муньков (отв. ред.) и др.]   244 с.
(...Вып. 80). — Библиогр. в примеч. в конце статей. — 600 экз. 1 р. 20 к.
В пер. — [70-47001ж]   9(470.41) + [016.3]

Fig. 2.

Translations:

43797. *Smirnova G. E.* Basic directions of contemporary bourgeois
philosophy. Lecture for a course of philosophy. [Leningrad], 1970. 16 pp.
(Ministry of Higher and Middle Special Education of the RSFSR. Leningrad
Polytechnical Institute named after M. I. Kalinin). Bibliography: pp. 15—16.
21cm. 1,000 copies. 10 kopeks. [70-66412] 1st impression. 1(104)(075.8)+
[016.3]

43798. *Mkryan M. M.* Movses Khorenatsi. Erevan, 'Aiastan', 1970. 230 pp.
In the Armenian language. 21cm. 5,000 copies. 66 kopeks. In hard cover.
[70-28994] 1st impression. 90(479.25)(092) Khorenatsi.

43803. *German* history in recent and latest times. In 2 vols. Editorial
board: S. D. Skazkin [and others]. Moscow, 'Nauka', 1970. (Academy of
Sciences of the USSR, Institute of General History). 22cm. Vol. 1 [Authors
M. M. Smirin, S. D. Skazkin and L. I. Gintsberg]. 510 pp. with illus.; 3 leaves
illus. and maps. 4,500 copies. 2 roubles 15 kopeks. In hard cover. [70-64034]
1st impression. 9(430)

43811. *From the history* of Tataria. [Symposium of articles]. Kazan',
1970. (Ministry of Education of the RSFSR. Kazan' State Pedagogical
Institute. Scholarly transactions . . .). 22cm. Symposium 4. [Editorial

board: ... N. M. Mun'kov (responsible editor) and others]. 244 pp. (...
Issue 80). Bibliography and notes at end of articles. 600 copies. 1 rouble
20 kopeks. In hard cover. [70-47001zh]. 9(470.41)+[016.3]

Indexes to both issues are published in separate quarterly numbers, each
containing name, geographical and (in the basic issue) subject indexes. There
is an annual index to series (Указатель серийных изданий), published
separately for each issue. References in all these indexes are only to item
number, which can often necessitate the chasing of several item numbers
back to weekly issues in search of further details.

4.1.2. Ежегодник книги (Ezhegodnik knigi: 'Annual of the book'). An
annual publication, cumulating the entries in the basic issue *only* of Книжная
летопись, and further excluding irregular series of the 'труды' type without
individual titles (these are recorded in the Летопись периодических
изданий — see 4.1.4).

Arrangement is into the same 31 subject classes as in Книжная летопись,
but since 1957 *EK* has appeared each year in two volumes of which the first
contains classes 1–14 and 23–31 (*ie* the humanities and social sciences), and
the second classes 15–22 (the natural sciences and technology).

Layout of entries is an abbreviated version of that in *KL*, and may contain
the elements listed there as 1–8, 10 (at end of entry), 12 and 13.

Indexes are given in each volume for: names; titles (only those occurring
as headings, *ie* when the author is not shown on the title-page); works in non-
Russian languages; translations; and subjects.

4.1.3. Новые книги СССР (Novye knigi SSSR: 'New books of the USSR').
A weekly, selective catalogue of forthcoming books, intended as a tool for
selection by non-Soviet buyers, and as such of great value due to the difficulty
of obtaining Soviet books even immediately after publication. It gives a far
from comprehensive picture of works in preparation, emphasising books
expected to appeal to readers abroad, giving very limited coverage of those
published outside Moscow and Leningrad and in languages other than Russian,
and excluding many titles published by the important publishing-house of the
Academy of Sciences of the USSR, 'Наука' (these are listed in separate annual
or semi-annual advance catalogues). There are no indexes. Alterations in

title, price and publication date are notified periodically, and occasional lists of cancelled titles appear. The length of advance notice varies greatly in practice, but appears to be intended as an average of around four months.

Arrangement is chiefly by subject classes, but under a system rather different from that of *KL* and *EK*. There are sometimes special sections, and occasionally special issues, devoted to a single publishing house or subject. The headings most regularly occurring are:

— Содержание ('Contents').

— Срочная информация ('Quick information': works just published and not previously announced, often in connection with special occasions such as Party congresses).

— Готовятся к выпуску ('Being prepared for issue').

— — Общественно-политическая и социально-экономическая литература ('Socio-political and socio-economic literature': includes history, politics, economics and planning).

— — Естественные науки. Математика ('Natural sciences. Mathematics').

— — Техника. Промышленность. Транспорт ('Technology. Industry. Transport').

— — Научные непериодические продолжающиеся издания ('Scholarly, irregular continuing publications': труды, сборники, etc., in numbered series).

— — Сельское хозяйство ('Agriculture').

— — Здравоохранение. Медицина ('Public health. Medicine').

— — Физическая культура. Спорт ('Physical culture. Sport').

— — Детская литература ('Childrens' literature').

— — Наука. Культура. Просвещение ('Scholarship. Culture. Education': includes linguistics, dictionaries and phrase books).

— — Художественная литература. Литературоведение ('Literature. Literary studies').

— — Искусство ('Art': includes theatre and cinema).

— — Печать. Книговедение. Библиотечное дело. Библиография ('The press. Study of books. Librarianship. Bibliography').

— — Учебная литература ('Educational literature': textbooks and instructional material. Includes sections on matter for language-learning).

— — Музыкальная литература ('Musical literature').

—— Изобразительная продукция ('Illustrative publications': *eg* reproductions, collections of illustrations).

— Вышли из печати. Публикуются впервые ('Issued from the press. Published for the first time': often from provincial or specialised publishinghouses).

— Публикуются повторно ('Published again': proposed reprintings, including those of titles not originally listed in *NK*, arranged by publisher).

— Информация ('Information': often announcements of major new multivolume works for subscription).

— Cancellations and alterations, shown as follows:

ВНИМАНИЮ КНИГОТОРГОВЫХ ФИРМ И ОРГАНИЗАЦИЙ!

Перечисленные ниже издания, опубликованные в 1966—1970 гг. в бюллетенях «Новые книги СССР» (НК), тематических каталогах «Советские книги» (СК) изданы не будут.

Fig. 3.

Translation: For the attention of book-trading firms and organisations! The publications listed below, announced in the years 1966–70 in the bulletins 'Novyi knigi SSSR' (NK), [and] the thematic catalogues 'Sovetskie knigi' (SK), will not be published.

ИЗМЕНЕНИЯ В НАЗВАНИИ, ОБЪЕМЕ И СТОИМОСТИ КНИГ

Fig. 4.

Translation: Changes in the titles, sizes and prices of books.

Layout of entries. Each main entry gives as many of the following elements as necessary:

1. Author.
2. Title and sub-title.
3. Language where other than Russian.
4. Publisher.
5. Anticipated size in 'sheets' (листы – each usually the equivalent of 16 printed pages).
6. Number of copies to be printed.

7. Anticipated price.

8. Expected date of publication, to the nearest quarter-year.

9. Descriptive paragraph on subject, treatment and intended readership.

10. Reference number, to be used when ordering.

Example:

Ч е р н ы й О. **Немецкая трагедия**. Повесть о Карле Либк-
нехте. (03). Политиздат. 20 л. с илл. В переплете. (Серия
«Пламенные революционеры»). 200.000 экз. 85 к. II квартал
1971 г.

> Основные вехи напряженного повествования таковы: Либкнехт
> в рейхстаге один против всех бросает свое «Нет!» войне: Либк-
> нехт — солдат рабочего батальона на фронте, жертва откровенной
> мести правых; Либкнехт ведет берлинских пролетариев на демонст-
> рацию; Либкнехт на скамье подсудимых, выступает как смелый обви-
> нитель; Либкнехт в каторжной тюрьме; Либкнехт и Роза Люксем-
> бург трагически погибают от руки наемников.
>
> В 1971 г. исполняется сто лет со дня рождения Карла Либкнех-
> та. В связи с этим книга будет особенно интересна широкому
> кругу читателей.

НК № 51—70 г.   (8)

Fig. 5.

Translation:

Chernyi O. *German tragedy*. The story of Karl Liebknecht. (03). Publishing
House for Political Literature. 20 sheets with illustrations. In hard cover.
(Series 'Ardent revolutionaries'). 200,000 copies. 85 kopeks. 2nd quarter of
1971. [. . . descriptive paragraph . . .]. NK No. 51-70(8)

4.1.4. Летопись периодических изданий СССР (Letopis' periodicheskikh
izdanii SSR: 'Chronicle of periodical publications of the USSR'). Since 1950,
a 5-yearly (for 1955–60, 6-yearly) bibliography of regular and irregular serials
published in the USSR during the quinquennium concerned. There are two
annual supplements: Летопись периодических изданий СССР. Новые,
переименованные и прекращенные изданием журналы и газеты (. . .
'New, renamed and discontinued journals and newspapers') and Летопись
периодических изданий СССР. Труды, ученые записки, сборники и
другие продолжающиеся издания (. . . 'Proceedings, scholarly transactions,
symposia and other serial publications'). These supplements are cumulated
into the 5-yearly volumes, together with material for the final year of the
quinquennium.

56

Journals with a small circulation, works newspapers, etc., are excluded, but serials of the труды type are covered comprehensively, including those listed in Книжная летопись.

Arrangement of the 5-yearly publication is into two volumes (части, 'parts'). Part I (Журналы, 'journals') is arranged internally by subject, Part II (Газеты, 'newpapers') by place of publication.

Layout of entries shows date from which published, any breaks in publication, and number of copies appearing during the period covered.

Indexes. Part I: title, language (where non-Russian), issuing body, place and title abbreviations, and place of publication. Part II: title, language and geographical.

4.1.5. Нотная ле́топись (Notnaya letopis': 'Chronicle of music'). Before 1967 Летопись музыкальной литературы. Quarterly bibliography of music published in the USSR.

4.1.6. Летопись печатных произведений изобразительного искусства (Letopis' pechatnykh proizvedenii izobrazitel'nogo iskusstva: 'Chronicle of printed works of illustrative art'). Before 1967 Летопись изобразительного искусства. Quarterly bibliography of original printed graphic works, published reproductions, photographs and posters.

4.1.7. Картографическая летопись (Kartograficheskaya letopis': 'Cartographic chronicle'). Annual bibliography of atlases and separately-published maps.

4.1.8. Летопись журнальных статей (Letopis' zhurnal'nykh statei: 'Chronicle of journal articles'). Weekly index to articles in journals, symposia and труды published in the USSR *in Russian*. About 1,000 journal titles are now represented in each issue, with the emphasis on scholarly material. Subject arrangement, quarterly name and geographical indexes. Annual supplement indexes source titles: Летопись журнальных статей. Список журналов и сборников, статьи из которых зарегистрированы в... году (. . . 'List of journals and symposia from which articles [were] indexed in the year . . .').

4.1.9. Летопись газетных статей (Letopis' gazetnykh statei: 'Chronicle of newspaper articles'). Selective monthly index to articles, documents and literary works published in Russian in about 40 Soviet newspapers. Subject arrangement, quarterly name and geographical indexes.

4.1.10. Летопись рецензий (Letopis' retsenzii: 'Chronicle of reviews'). Quarterly bibliography of reviews published in the periodicals indexed by Летопись журнальных статей and Летопись газетных статей (4.1.8 and 4.1.9), and in certain local papers. Reviews may be of works in any language, published in the USSR or elsewhere. Classified arrangement by the subject of the original book, a short bibliographical description of which is followed by details of the reviews dealing with it. Each issue has author, editor and title indexes to the books reviewed (separately listed for Soviet and non-Soviet publications) and a name index of reviewers. Indexes are cumulated in the fourth issue of each year.

4.1.11. Реферативный журнал (Referativnyi zhurnal: 'Abstracts journal') consists of — in 1972 — 170 separate abstracting journals published at monthly or twice-monthly intervals by VINITI (ВИНИТИ), the All-Union Institute for Scientific and Technical Information. Each of the 170 'issues' (выпуски) covers articles, patents, monographs, etc. published all over the world in a given field of science or technology. The entire enterprise represents the largest single abstracting organisation in the world. Twenty five 'combined volumes' (сводные томы) are also published, containing between them 132 'issues' of the total 170. Annual indexes are produced for all combined volumes and single issues.

All issues available for subscription are described in VINITI's annual catalogue and in a supplement to 'Periodicals of the USSR' (see 5.1). A detailed guide in English to content and use is: COPLEY, E. J. *A guide to Referativnyi zhurnal.* 2nd ed. revised. London, National Reference Library of Science and Invention, 1972.

4.2. RETROSPECTIVE BIBLIOGRAPHIES AND CATALOGUES
Retrospective identification of Russian and Soviet publications is catered for (apart from back runs of the works listed in 4.1), by a large number of bibliographies and catalogues, which nevertheless, even taken together, do not

provide a total coverage. Most of the works concerned are listed with notes and comment in:

4.2.1. MAICHEL, K. *Guide to Russian reference books. Ed. by J. S. G. Simmons. Vol. 1: General bibliographies and reference works. Vol. 2: History, ethnography, geography. Vol. 5: Science, technology, medicine.* [No more publ.] . Stanford, Hoover Inst., 1962–67.

4.2.2. HORECKY, P. L. *Basic Russian publications. An annotated bibliography on Russia and the Soviet Union.* Chicago, UP, 1962.

4.2.3. HORECKY, P. L. *Russia and the Soviet Union: a bibliographical guide to Western-language publications.* Chicago, UP, 1965.

The most easily usable large catalogue, and one of the most comprehensive (though this is still a very relative term) is:

4.2.4. NEW YORK. PUBLIC LIBRARY. REFERENCE DEPT. *Dictionary catalogue of the Slavonic collection.* Boston, G. K. Hall, 1959. 26 vols.
This gives name and subject entries for a collection of about 120,000 volumes on and from the Slavonic countries. Of books not in English, 65% are in Russian. Medicine, theology and law are less extensively represented than other subjects.

Two other, more widely available general catalogues containing much Russian-language material are:

4.2.5. The various cumulations of the Library of Congress' *National Union catalog*, and

4.2.6. The British Museum's *General catalogue of printed books* and its supplements.

These latter three catalogues all include serial titles, but a large number of these are conveniently brought together in:

4.2.7. SMITS, R. *Half a century of Soviet serials 1917–1968. A bibliography and union list of serials published in the USSR.* Washington, Library of Congress, 1968. 2 vols.
This lists both regular and irregular serials, except those in Oriental languages, with a thorough statement of issues published in each case. It is being supplemented by:

4.2.8. SCHATOFF, M. *Half a century of Russian serials 1917–1968. Cumulative index of serials published outside the USSR. Ed. by N. A. Hale.* New York, Russian Book Chamber Abroad, 1970–72. 4 vols.

4.3. QUICK-REFERENCE WORKS IN ENGLISH

Encyclopedias. There is no up-to-date encyclopedia in English devoted exclusively to Russia and the USSR. The first three titles below are still handy compendia, but can usefully be supplemented by articles in more modern general encyclopedias.

4.3.1. UTECHIN, S. V., *ed. Everyman's concise encyclopedia of Russia.* London, Dent, 1961.
Still useful, though now outdated in its bibliographies (English-language only) and in many articles on the contemporary USSR.

4.3.2. FLORINSKY, M. T., *ed. McGraw-Hill encyclopedia of Russia and the Soviet Union.* New York, McGraw, 1961.
Similar coverage to 4.3.1, and similarly suffers now from its date of publication.

4.3.3. Information USSR. Oxford, Pergamon, 1962.
Expanded and updated, but basically a translation of vol. 50 of the 2nd ed. of the *Bol'shaya sovetskaya éntsiklopediya,* which is devoted entirely to the USSR in all its aspects.

Atlas

4.3.4. Atlas SSSR. 2-e izd. Moskva, GUGK, 1969.
An exception to the 'in English' in the heading of this section, but worth inclusion as a well-produced, up-to-date atlas of the Soviet Union.

Directory

4.3.5. World of learning. Europa. Annual.
Section on the USSR gives brief data on academies, learned societies, archives, libraries, museums, universities and other higher educational and research institutions. Addresses, and often leading members of staff, are shown.

Biographical dictionaries

4.3.6. Prominent personalities in the USSR. Metuchen, NJ, Scarecrow, 1968.
Over 6,000 biographies of leading *living* Soviet figures in all fields of activity. Appendix of important personnel arranged by organisation. Successor to *Who's who in the USSR.*

4.3.7. CROWLEY, E. L., *ed. Party and government officials of the Soviet Union 1917–1967.* Metuchen, NJ, Scarecrow, 1969.

'Party officials' section covers period from foundation of RSDRP in 1898. Traces membership of Central Committee and top specialist committees, with full lists and notes of intervening changes, arranged chronologically by congress. Ch. 2 (Government) is arranged by post. Various CPSU statistics and organisational schemes appended. Name and general indexes.

Abstracts and digests

4.3.8. ABSEES. *Soviet and East European abstracts series.* University of Glasgow, 1970– . Quarterly.

Abstracts of books, journal and newspaper articles from the USSR and other E. European countries. Wide subject coverage, but excluding pure science and most technology. Detailed subject arrangement, annual indexes.

4.3.9. Current digest of the Soviet press. Columbus, AAASS, 1949– Weekly.

Selected contents of over 60 major Soviet newspapers and journals, translated or condensed. Weekly indexes to *Pravda* and *Izvestiya,* quarterly general cumulative indexes.

Literary dictionary

4.3.10. The Penguin companion to literature. 2: European. Ed. by A. Thorlby. Harmondsworth, Penguin, 1969.

Useful, up-to-date work with articles on 175 Russian writers and separate treatment of periods and movements. Select bibliographies follow each article.

4.4. RUSSIAN-ENGLISH DICTIONARIES

4.4.1. SMIRNITSKII, A. I. *Russian-English dictionary. 7th ed.* Moscow, 'Soviet Encyclopedia', 1965.

New impressions and editions appear at intervals. For many years the standard Russian-English dictionary. About 50,000 words.

4.4.2. Russko-angliiskii slovar'. Sost. A. M. Taube [i dr.]. Moskva, 1965. About 35,000 words. Intended for learners of English.

4.4.3. *The Oxford Russian-English dictionary. By M. Wheeler.* OUP, 1972.
New dictionary, likely to become the standard work for general use.
About 70,000 entries.

4.4.4. *Dictionary of spoken Russian: Russian-English, English-Russian.*
New York, Dover, 1958.
Reprint of US War Department manual. Deals with the (then) current
colloquial language, emphasising the use of words in context.

4.4.5. LIBRARY OF CONGRESS. AEROSPACE TECHNOLOGY DIVISION.
REFERENCE DEPT. *Glossary of Russian abbreviations and acronyms.*
Washington, Library of Congress, 1967.
About 23,600 entries, restricted to abbreviations of 20th century and
acronyms from 1945. Some emphasis on aerospace technology. Each
entry gives expansion and translation.

4.4.6. *Slovar' sokrashchenii russkogo yazyka.* Moskva, Gos. izd-vo inostr. i
nats. slovarei, 1963.
No English, but useful for obsolete abbreviations and more handy
than 4.4.5.

4.4.7. CROWE, B. *Concise dictionary of Soviet terminology, institutions
and abbreviations.* Oxford, Pergamon, 1969.
About 1,700 'Sovietisms', emphasising those most common in Soviet
literature, with explanations designed for English readers.

4.4.8. SMITH, R. E. F. *A Russian-English dictionary of social science terms.*
London, Butterworths, 1962.
Covers sociology, politics, economics, public administration and
education. Over 9,000 entries.

4.4.9. PUSHKAREV, S. G. *Dictionary of Russian historical terms from the
11th century to 1917.* Yale UP, 1970.
Terminology of politics, law, society, economics, finance, taxation,
offices and ranks. Many definitions are long, with historical explanations and quotations. About 1,500 terms.

4.4.10. ALFORD, M. H. T. *and* ALFORD, V. L. *Russian-English scientific
and technical dictionary.* Oxford, Pergamon, 1970. 2 vols.
Over 100,000 entries.

5. NOTES ON ACQUISITION

Difficulties in the acquisition of material in Russian arise for several reasons: the speed with which many new Soviet titles become, in practice, 'out of print'; the difficulty of a library's ordering direct from the USSR commercially and the limited number of dealers outside the USSR with adequate stocks and expertise in handling Soviet titles; the delays and uncertainties often associated with exchange agreements; the increasing demand for out-of-print scholarly material in Russian, creating scarcity and high prices; and the variety of alternatives to an original copy which are now appearing for an increasing range of titles, thanks to microforms and the many different techniques of full-size reproduction.

Notes are given below on sources of supply for original copies and reproductions of material in Russian.

5.1. ORIGINAL PUBLICATIONS

The most reliable method of obtaining new Soviet publications is, unsurprisingly, to order in advance from an experienced supplier — whether a dealer or an exchange partner. For comment on *Novye knigi SSSR* as a source of advance information, see 4.1.3. Besides the advance catalogues of 'Nauka', which give notice of titles not included in *Novye knigi SSSR*, the annual plans (тематические планы or темпланы) of certain other Soviet publishing houses are distributed outside the USSR. Although the titles they forecast will normally appear in *NK*, they have the advantage of showing an entire year's publishing programme, subject though this will be to modifications, delays and cancellations. Periodicals available on subscription to customers abroad (again via dealers or exchange partners) are listed in an annual catalogue, Газеты и журналы СССР (English title: 'Periodicals of the USSR').

Acquiring titles even recently published can often require speculative approaches to several suppliers. The older the item, the smaller the number of copies printed, the more remote its place of publication, and the less acceptable its political and social standpoint in the USSR of today, the more probable it becomes that one will need to be satisfied with something other than an original copy.

63

5.1.1. Purchase and subscription from the British, European and American
book trade.

A relatively small number of dealers have wide experience of trading in
Russian-language and Soviet material, and even fewer are permitted by
'Mezhdunarodnaya Kniga', the Soviet book export organisation, to deal with
it direct in ordering new publications. Prices charged by dealers for new Soviet
publications will usually be appreciably higher than a direct conversion of the
price given in *Novye knigi SSSR* would suggest. Books are often published at
a higher price than that quoted in *NK*, which is only intended as an indication
of price level. Besides this frequent price increase 'at source', 'Mezhdunarodnaya
Kniga' includes a percentage surcharge, which varies with the type of work,
in its price to dealers. Beyond this point, individual dealers will each have
their own practices with respect to profit margins.

The list below shows firms known to handle Russian and East European
material regularly. Specialities are indicated for a few where works in Russian
are not emphasised. All firms distribute their own catalogues of new and/or
antiquarian holdings.

Great Britain

Blackwells, 48/51 Broad Street, Oxford OX1 3BQ. Tel. Oxford 49111.
Telex 83118.

Bowes & Bowes, 1/2 Trinity Street, Cambridge CB2 1SX. Tel. Cambridge
55488.

K. J. Bredon's Bookshop, 10 East St., Brighton BN1 1HP. Tel. Brighton
29577.

Bristol Slavonic Titles, 7 Ploughed Paddock, Nailsea, Somerset. Tel.
Nailsea 3452.

Central Books Ltd., 37 Grays Inn Rd., London WC1X 8PS. Tel.
01-242 6166.

Collets Holdings Ltd., Denington Estate, Wellingborough, Northants.
Tel. Wellingborough 4351.

Collets Russian Bookshop, 39 Museum St., London WC1A 1LS. Tel.
01-405 5142.

Cracovia Book Co., 58 Pembroke Rd., London W8 6NY. Tel. 01-603 3647.
(Polish material).

Earlscourt Publications Ltd., 130 Shepherds Bush Centre, London W12. Tel. 01-749 3097 and 01-743 2391. (Polish material).

F.C.I. Book Service, 4 Holland Rd., London W14 8BA. Tel. 01-367 8252. (Czechoslovak material).

H. Fellner, 70 Gascony Ave., London NW6 4NE. Tel. 01-624 5417.

Anthony C. Hall, 30 Staines Rd., Twickenham, Middx. Tel. 01-898 2638.

Hammersmith Bookshop, Liffords Place, High St., London SW13. Tel. 01-770 7254.

W. Heffer & Sons Ltd., 20 Trinity St., Cambridge. Tel. Cambridge 58351. Telex 81298 HEFFER CAMBRIDGE.

Holdan Books, 121 London Rd., Headington, Oxford OX3 9HZ. Tel. Oxford 65384.

Interpress Ltd., 179A Blythe Rd., London W14 0HL. Tel. 01-603 6819. (Czechoslovak material).

Iskander, 12 McGregor Rd., London W11 1DE.

K Books, Fremington, Richmond, Yorks. Tel. Reeth 404.

Ben Kane Book Service, 27–29 Amwell St., London EC1R 1UN. Tel. 01-837 8025.

R. W. Malynowsky, 18 Doughty St., London WC1N 2PL.

Prideaux Press, Icknield Way, Letchworth, Herts, SG6 4AD. Tel. Letchworth 4499.

Publishing & Distributing Co., Ltd., Mitre House, 177 Regent St., London W1R 8HR. Tel. 01-734 2361.

Europe, Asia and America

Librairie Academia, 9 av. Henri-Dunant, 1211 Genève 4, Switzerland.

Johannes Alt, 6000 Frankfurt 70, Gartenstr. 134, Postfach 70/0104, Germany.

Aticot Antiquarian Booksellers, 20 Shenkin Str., Tel Aviv, Israel.

E. J. Brill, Oude Rijn 33A, Leiden, Netherlands.

Brücken Verlag, 4000 Düsseldorf, Ackerstr. 3, Postschliessfach 1928, Germany.

A. Buschke, 80 East 11th St., New York, NY 10003, USA.

I. Chmeljuk, 1 rue de Fleurus, Paris 6e, France.

Librarie des Cinq Continents, 18 rue de Lille, Paris 6e, France.

Davies Book Co. Ltd., 2220 Beaconsfield Ave., Montreal 261, P.Q., Canada.

Deecee Books, P.O. Box 506, Nyack, NY 10960, USA.

Four Continent Book Corp., 156 Fifth Ave., New York, NY 10010, USA.

Robert Fricke, 1 Berlin 12, Charlottenburg, Hardenbergpl. 13, Germany.

H. Geyer, A-1061 Wien, Hofmühlg. 14, Austria.

Dr. Rudolf Habelt, 53 Bonn 5, Am Buchenhang 1, Germany.

Otto Harrassowitz, 62 Wiesbaden, Taunusstr. 5, Germany.

Hans Hartinger Nachf., 1 Berlin 15, Xantenerstr. 14, Germany.

J. J. Heckenhauer, 74 Tübingen, Holzmarkt 5, Germany.

L. Heidrich, 1010 Wien, Plankeng. 7, Austria. (Czechoslovakia and Austria-Hungary).

Das Internationale Buch, Wien 1, Trattnerhof 1, Austria.

Journalfranz Arnulf Liebing, 87 Würzburg 2, Postfach 1136, Germany.

Victor Kamkin, Inc., 12224 Parklawn Drive, Rockville, Md. 20852, USA.

Boris Kaplanski, 8 rue du Loing, Paris 14e, France.

B. Kirilloff, 18bis rue du Gén. Delestraint, Paris 16e, France.

Kubon & Sagner, 8 München 34, Schliessfach 68, Germany.

Les Livres Étrangers, 10 rue Armand Moisant, Paris 15e, France.

Philip Lozinski, 1504 Drift Rd., Westport, Mass. 02790, USA, and 4763 Victoria Ave., Montreal 247, P.Q., Canada.

Mercurius Books & Periodicals, 36 Unque Place, Amityville, L.I., NY 11701, USA.

A. Neimanis, 8 München 2, Linprunstr. 11, Germany.

Martinus Nijhoff, Lange Voorhout 9, The Hague, Netherlands.

Jan Peet, POB 3743, Amsterdam, Netherlands.

Pegasus, Leidsestraat 25, Amsterdam, Netherlands.

Russian-American Book Agency 'VEK', 602 West 139th St., New York, NY 10031, USA.

Russian Language Specialists, Box 4546, Chicago, Ill. 60680, USA.

Russian National Bookstore, 321 East 14th St., New York, NY 10003, USA.

George Sabo Slavic Books, 2400 N.AIA, Melbourne, Fla. 32901, USA.

Smolders, 1162 Wien, POB 29, Austria. (Czechoslovakia and Austria-Hungary).

W. P. van Stockum NV, Buitenhof 36, The Hague, Netherlands.

Dr. R. Trofenik, 8 München 13, Elisabethstr. 18, Germany. (SE Europe).

Zentralantiquariat der DDR, 701 Leipzig, Talstr. 29, Postf. 1080, German Democratic Republic.

5.1.2. Exchanges with libraries and other institutions in the USSR.

In the present supply situation, it is probably true to say that libraries requiring only a limited number of Soviet books and journals, which are recent titles from major publishing houses, would find commercial channels preferable to exchanges as a means of acquisition. Exchange partners vary greatly in enthusiasm and reliability, though most of the larger Soviet libraries are well used to exchange transactions. Partners can be extremely valuable in procuring out-of-print books and back runs of serials and irregular series which are unobtainable in the original through other channels, but prices for exchange purposes are determined fairly uniformly, and for pre-1945 publications are high even by Western standards. The two types of Western library likely to benefit most from exchanges are, firstly, the large library requiring older or more obscure publications on an appreciable scale and with the budget to afford them: it is easier for large libraries to bear the fluctuating financial demands of an exchange agreement. Secondly, the highly-specialised library may be able to find similarly specialised partners with access to material hard to acquire commercially — particularly if the 'home' library can offer desirable publications of its own. Exchanges on a 'value-for-value' basis are usually acceptable to Soviet libraries (which, however, usually prefer a title-for-title or volume-for-volume basis if the partner is willing).

5.1.3. Inter-library loans of books and journals in Russian from British and foreign libraries.

For scientific and technical books and journals, and journals only in the social sciences and humanities, the National Lending Library for Science and Technology at Boston Spa is the primary lending source in the UK. Applications for books in the social sciences and humanities are usually best made through the Slavonic Union Catalogue at the National Central Library, which will also move to Boston Spa in 1973, to form part of the British Library, and will, where necessary, forward applications abroad to the Soviet Union and elsewhere. Many libraries, including some large libraries in Western Europe, will accept direct applications for loans. Information on British collections of Russian and East European material is contained in:

WALKER, G., *et al., eds. Directory of libraries and special collections on Eastern Europe and the USSR.* London, Crosby Lockwood, Hamden, Conn., Archon, 1971.

5.1.4. Duplicates from other libraries. Most libraries collecting material in Russian acquire duplicates over the years (chiefly owing to the identification difficulties dealt with in 3.2.4 and 3.6!). Few have time to prepare and circulate lists, but will usually be happy for a visitor to make his selection on the spot. Disposal may be free, at some proportion of the original cost, or by exchange.

5.2. COPIES

5.2.1. Commercially-published reprints, microforms and photocopies. Many publishers are now issuing books and journals in Russian in one or more of these forms of reproduction. Concentration has tended to be on large reference and bibliographical works, back runs of scholarly and literary journals, and treatises of recognised academic worth. Some publishers have embarked on very large copying projects (*eg* on Russian and Soviet legal materials, and Russian books of the 18th century), in some cases using the resources of Soviet libraries. There is at present no comprehensive guide to commercial reproductions. For those produced up to 1965, see:

MAY, M., *and* THIKIAN, A. *Ouvrages cyrilliques concernant les sciences sociales et humaines: liste de réproductions disponibles.* (Cahiers du monde russe et soviétique, suppl. 1–2). Paris, Mouton, 1964–65. 2 vols.

A more complete list is currently (1972) being compiled in card catalogue form at Cambridge University Library. For published guides after 1965, the annual *Guide* and *Subject guide to microforms in print*, and the annual *Guide to reprints* and quarterly *Announced reprints* may be consulted, together with publishers' own prospectuses.

5.2.2. 'Home-made' copies of works held in, or borrowed from, other libraries. The question of copyright does not normally arise in copying Soviet publications since the USSR is not a signatory of the Berne or Universal Copyright Conventions. However, works in Russian published elsewhere (*eg* in the USA, France, Western Germany or the UK) may well be subject to copyright restrictions, and the position should be checked before copying to any greater extent than that allowed by 'fair dealing' provisions.

6. IDENTIFICATION OF OTHER EAST EUROPEAN LANGUAGES

6.1. RUSSIAN AND OTHER EAST EUROPEAN LANGUAGES

Besides being the native language of a majority of the population of the USSR, *Russian* is the standard medium of communication throughout that country for academic, political and administrative purposes above the local level; hence it is the language used in the bulk of Soviet writing of any significance to readers outside the Soviet Union, particularly on scientific and technical topics.

Of the other languages recognised in the Soviet Union, six in the European part of the country appear in a considerable volume of publications, each being the major indigenous language of one of the USSR's constituent republics. *Ukrainian* and *Belorussian* are closely related to Russian, and together these three are regarded as the eastern sub-group of the *Slavonic* or *Slavic* group of languages. *Lithuanian* and *Lettish*, spoken in the Soviet Socialist Republics of Lithuania and Latvia respectively, are the only two survivors of the *Baltic* group of languages which shows many similarities to the Slavonic group. *Estonian* has little resemblance to any European language except Finnish, spoken on the other side of the Baltic. *Moldavian*, spoken in the south-western corner of the USSR, is closely related to *Romanian*, just across the frontier, and both are an offshoot of the Romance group of languages which includes Italian and French.

Defining 'Eastern Europe' (apart from the USSR) as comprising Poland, Czechoslovakia, Hungary, Jugoslavia, Bulgaria, Romania, Albania and the German Democratic Republic (the DDR) – in other words, those countries where this group would normally be described as the 'socialist states' of Europe – we find languages with widely differing affinities, but with those of the Slavonic group predominating. The West Slavonic sub-group covers *Polish*; *Czech* and *Slovak* (spoken in western and eastern Czechoslovakia respectively); and *Lusatian*, also called *Sorb* and *Wendish*, spoken by a Slavonic minority in the DDR. The South Slavonic languages are *Serbo-Croat*, *Slovene* and *Macedonian*, all occurring in Jugoslavia, and *Bulgarian*.

Hungarian is a language with little resemblance to its neighbours or to languages elsewhere in Europe, having been established in the continent by a people emigrating from further east in the early middle ages. It is spoken by minorities in Slovakia, Romania and Jugoslavia, as well as in Hungary itself. *Albanian* is spoken in Albania and by a sizeable minority in Jugoslavia, and shows little likeness to the Slavonic and Greek which surround it. *Romanian* has been mentioned earlier as a Romance language. The standard *German* usage of the DDR is, at least at present, more or less identical with that of the western Federal Republic of Germany.

The table below shows schematically the relationship between the Slavonic languages, and the alphabets and number of speakers for all the East European languages. Figures are taken from:

GILYAREVSKY, R. S., *and* GRIVNIN, V. S. *Languages identification guide.* Moscow, Nauka, 1970.

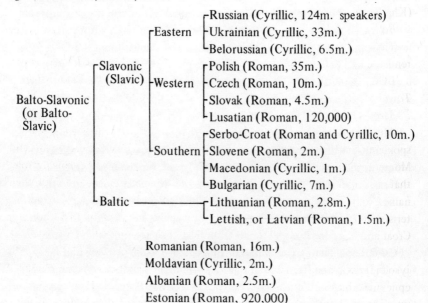

Romanian (Roman, 16m.)
Moldavian (Cyrillic, 2m.)
Albanian (Roman, 2.5m.)
Estonian (Roman, 920,000)
Hungarian (Roman, 13m.)

6.2. IDENTIFICATION GUIDE

For each East European language, the list below gives recognition features in alphabet and orthography, vernacular names for the nationalities and localities concerned, and the towns most frequently occurring as places of publication.

6.2.1. Languages using the Cyrillic alphabet

Russian

ы occurs only in Russian and Belorussian, while Belorussian does not use и. CCCP: USSR. советский: Soviet (adj.). Россия, российский: Russia, Russian (of the country, especially pre-1917). русский: Russian (of the language and people). *Towns*: Москва (Moscow). Ленинград (Leningrad). See also the classified vocabulary in 7.2.22.

Ukrainian

The letters є and ï are peculiar to the language. i now occurs only in Ukrainian and Belorussian.

УРСР: Ukrainian SSR (not the *Union* of Soviet Socialist Republics). Україна, український: Ukraine, Ukrainian. *Towns:* Київ (Kiev). Харків (Khar'kov). Львів (L'vov).

Belorussian

The letter ў is peculiar to the language. и and щ are not used, being rendered by i and шч.

БССР: Belorussian SSR. Беларусь, беларускі: Belorussia, Belorussian. *Town:* Мінск (Minsk).

Serbo-Croat

Although to all intents and purposes the same language, the Serbo-Croat spoken in the Jugoslav constituent republics of Serbia, Bosnia-Hercegovina and Montenegro, is written in Cyrillic and often described simply as Serbian, while that spoken in the republic of Croatia uses the Roman alphabet and often the name Croato-Serbian, Croat or Croatian. In Cyrillic, Serbo-Croat is characterised by the letters ħ (ć) and ђ (đ). ј, љ, њ and џ are common to Serbo-Croat and Macedonian.

СФРЈ: Socialist Federal Republic of Jugoslavia. Југославија, југословенски:Jugoslavia, Jugoslav. српскохрватски: Serbo-Croat. Србија, српски:Serbia, Serbian. Босна, босански: Bosnia, Bosnian. Црна Гора, црногорски: Montenegro, Montenegrin. *Towns:* Београд (Belgrade). Нови Сад (Novi Sad). Сарајево (Sarajevo). Ниш (Niš). Приштина (Priština). Титоград (Titograd). Цетиње (Cetinje). Пећ (Peć).

Macedonian

ѓ, s and ќ are peculiar to the language. ј, љ, њ and џ occur in Macedonian and Serbo-Croat only. Definite articles are added as suffixes to the *end* of a

71

noun or adjective as they are in Bulgarian. In Macedonian, they are most often -от, -та, -то or -те.

Македонија, македонски: Macedonia, Macedonian. *Town*: Скопје (Skopje).

Bulgarian

The letter ъ, while not unique to Bulgarian, now occurs far more frequently there (where it has roughly the sound of '-er' in 'bitter') than in any other language currently using Cyrillic. Suffixed definite articles occur as in Macedonian, their most frequent Bulgarian forms being -ът, -та, -то and -те.

НРБ: Peoples' Republic of Bulgaria. България, български: Bulgaria, Bulgarian. *Towns*: София (Sofia). Пловдив (Plovdiv). Варна (Varna).

Moldavian

The endings -у, -ул, -лор and -ре are characteristic, also the auxiliary words луй, ла, де, ши.

РССМ: Moldavian SSR. Молдова, молдовенеск: Moldavia, Moldavian. *Town*: Кишинэу (Kishinev).

6.2.2. *Languages using the Roman alphabet*

Polish

ź and ż are unique to Polish, ł and ś to Polish and Lusatian, ą and ę to Polish and Lithuanian. w instead of v is peculiar to Polish and Lusatian among the Slavonic languages.

PRL: Polish Peoples' Republic. Polska, polski: Poland, Polish. Śląsk, śląski: Silesia, Silesian. *Towns*: Warszawa (Warsaw). Kraków (Cracow). Gdańsk (*German* Danzig). Poznań. Wrocław (*German* Breslau). Lublin.

Czech

ů is unique to Czech, ě and ř occur only in Czech and Lusatian. The acute accent marking all long vowels (á, é, í, ó, ú, ý) is common to Czech and Slovak, as are the 'soft' consonants d', ď, ň, t' and ľ.

ČSSR: Czechoslovak Socialist Republic. ČSR: Czech Socialist Republic (up to 1939: Czechoslovak Republic). Československo: Czechoslovakia. Čechy, český: Bohemia, Bohemian (or Czech). Morava, moravský: Moravia, Moravian. Slezsko, slezský: Silesia, Silesian. *Towns*: Praha (Prague – v Praze: in Prague). Brno. Plzeň. Olomouc. Ostrava.

Slovak

l' is unique to the language. The acute accent marking long vowels, and the

72

'soft' consonants d', ď, ň, t' and ľ are common to Czech and Slovak. ä and ô do not occur in any other Slavonic language.

Slovensko, slovenský: Slovakia, Slovak (cf. Slovene). *Towns*: Bratislava. Košice. Martin.

Lusatian

ł and w appear as in Polish, and ě and ř as in Czech.

Łužica, łužiski: Lusatia, Lusatian. Serbja, serbski: Sorbia, Sorb; Lusatia, Lusatian. *Towns*: Budyšin (Bautzen). Chóśebuz (Kottbus).

Serbo-Croat

In Serbo-Croat in its Roman orthography, as used in Croatia and sometimes called Croato-Serbian, đ is unique. The combinations dj, ji, lj and nj are frequent.

Hrvatska, hrvatski: Croatia, Croatian. SFRJ: Socialist Federal Republic of Jugoslavia. Jugoslavija, jugoslovenski: Jugoslavia, Jugoslav. hrvatskosrpski: Croato-Serbian, Serbo-Croat. *Towns*: Zagreb. Rijeka. Split. Dubrovnik.

Slovene

No unique characters in the alphabet, which lacks, *eg*, Serbo-Croat đ and West Slavonic y. Note the word *in* ('and') instead of the more usual Slavonic *i*.

Slovenija, slovenski: Slovenia, Slovene (cf. Slovak). *Towns*: Ljubljana. Maribor.

Lithuanian

The letters ė, į and ų are unique to the language. *ir* = 'and'.

Lietuva, lietuvis: Lithuania, Lithuanian. *Towns:* Vilnins. Kaunas.

Lettish (Latvian)

Four long vowels are marked thus: ā, ē, ī, ū. ģ, ķ, ļ and ņ are also unique. *un* = 'and'.

Latvija, latvietis: Latvia, Latvian. *Town*: Rīga.

Romanian

ă, ş and ţ are unique. Endings -ea, -ul, -ului and -ilor are frequent.

RSR: Romanian Socialist Republic. România, românesc/românească: Romania, Romanian. *Towns*: Bucureşti (Bucharest). Braşov. Timişoara. Iaşi (Jassy). Cluj.

Albanian

ë, q and the combination xh are frequent and characteristic. *dhe* = 'and'.

Republika Popullore Shqipërisë: Peoples' Republic of Albania. Shqipëri, shqipe: Albania, Albanian. *Towns*: Tiranë (Tirana). Durrës. Shkodër. Peja (Peć, Jugoslavia). Prishtina (Priština, Jugoslavia).

73

Estonian

üü is unique to the language, and õ among East European languages.
Eesti, eesti: Estonia, Estonian. *Towns*: Tallinn. Tartu.

Hungarian

The unique long umlauted vowels ő and ű occur as well as the short ö and ü.
The consonant groups cs, gy, sz and zs are characteristic.

MNK: Hungarian Peoples' Republic. Magyarország, magyar: Hungary,
Hungarian. *Towns:* Budapest. Szeged. Debrecen. Pécs. Kolozsvár (Cluj,
Romania).

7. VOCABULARY

This section consists of (7.1) a guide to word-endings, (7.2) a classified
vocabulary arranged by subjects or categories to assist learning, and (7.3)
a complete Russian-to-English list of all Russian words and phrases used in
this book, and a selection of others.

7.1. GUIDE TO WORD ENDINGS

The grammatical form in which words are entered in these vocabularies (as in
dictionaries) is standardised as the nominative singular of nouns, the nominative
singular masculine of adjectives and the infinitive of verbs. The most common
variant endings are listed below, with a key to the form of ending which will
be found in the vocabulary and dictionary entry.

Ending	If not in dictionary, try under:	Grammatical explanation
none	-а, -о	noun: gen. pl. fem. or neut.
-а (see also -ла)	none or -о	noun: gen./acc. sg. masc., gen. sg. neut. or nom. pl. neut.
-ам	none, -а, -о	noun: dat. pl.
-ами	none, -а, -о	noun: instr. pl.
-ах	none, -а, -о	noun: loc. pl.
-ая	-ый	adj.: nom. sing. fem.
-е (see also -ее, -ие, -ое, ые)	none, -а, -я or -о	noun: loc. sing., or dat. sing. fem.
-его	-ий	adj.: gen./acc. sg. masc., gen. sg. neut.
-ее	-ый, -ий	adj.: comparative form or nom./acc. sg. neut.
-ей	-я, -ь, -е	noun: instr. sg. fem., or gen. pl. fem. or neut.

75

Ending	If not in dictionary, try under:	Grammatical explanation
-ем	{ -й, -е { -ий	noun: instr. sg. masc. or neut. adj.: loc. sing. masc. or neut.
-ему	-ий	adj.: dat. sg. masc./neut.
-и (see also -ими, -ки, -ли, -ыми)	none, -а, -я, -ь, -е	noun: gen. or loc. sg. fem., loc. sg. neut., nom./acc. pl. masc., nom. pl. fem.
-ие	-ий	adj.: nom./acc. pl.
-ий	-ия, -ие	noun: gen. pl. fem. or neut.
-им	-ий	adj.: instr. sg. masc./neut., dat. pl.
-ими	-ий	adj.: instr. pl.
-их	-ий	adj.: gen. or loc. pl., or acc. pl. masc.
-ки	-кий	adverb: derived from adj. (see 1.5.4)
-л, -ла, -ло, -ли, -лся, -лась, лось, -лись	-ть, ться	verb: past tense (see 1.10.3, 1.10.4)
-о (see also -его, -ло, -ого)	-ый	adverb: derived from adj. (see 1.5.4)
-ов	none	noun: gen./acc. pl. masc.
-ого	-ый	adj.: gen./acc. sg. masc. or gen. sg. neut.
-ое	-ый	adj.: nom./acc. sg. neut.
-ой	{ -ый { -а	adj.: gen./dat./instr./loc. sg. fem. noun: instr. sing. fem.
-ом	{ none or -о { -ый	noun: instr. sg. masc. or neut. adj.: loc. sg. masc. or neut.

Ending	If not in dictionary, try under:	Grammatical explanation
-ому	-ый	adj.: dat. sg. masc. or neut.
-у (see also -ему, -ому)	none, -о, -а	noun: dat. sg. masc. or neut., acc. sg. fem.
-ую	-ый	adj.: acc. sing. fem.
-ы	none, -а, -о	noun: nom. pl. masc. or fem., gen. sg. fem.
.-ые	-ый	adj.: nom./acc. pl.
-ым	-ый	adj.: instr. sg. masc. or neut., or dat. pl.
-ыми	-ый	adj.: instr. pl.
-ых	-ый	adj.: gen. pl. or acc. pl. masc.
-ью	-ь	noun: instr. sg. fem.
-ю (see also -ую, ью)	-я, -е	noun: acc. sg. fem., dat. sg. neut.
-я	-й, -е	noun: gen./acc. sg. masc., gen. sg. neut. or nom. pl. neut.
-ям	-й, -я, -ь, -е	noun: dat. pl.
-ями	-й, -я, -ь, -е	noun: instr. pl.
-ях	-й, -я, -ь, -е	noun: loc. pl.

7.2. CLASSIFIED VOCABULARY

1. Common conjunctions and adverbs.
2. Generalities.
3. Abbreviations.
4. Scholarship and culture.
5. Writing and authorship.
6. Types of publication.
7. The book: physical characteristics.
8. Publishing and the book trade.
9. Publishing houses in the USSR.
10. Bibliographic and reference work.
11. Education.
12. Politics and administration.
13. Economics and planning.
14. History.
15. The arts.

1. Common conjunctions and adverbs

а	and, but	но	but
где	where	так	so, thus
ещё	still, yet	также	also, as well
и	and	тоже	also, as well
или	or	только	only
как	how	уже	already
не	not		

2. Generalities

включать	(ipfve), включить (pfve) to include	задача	problem, task, object
вопрос	question, matter	значение	meaning, significance
всеобщий	universal, general		
выдающийся	prominent, distinguished	итог	sum, total; result
готовить	(ipfve) to prepare. (-ся) to be prepared	кончать	(ipfve), кончить (pfve) to finish, end. (-ся) be finished, ended.
дело	affair, matter, business		
деятель	functionary, worker; person, figure	краткий	short
		лёгкий	light, easy
		лучший	better, best
		люди	people
другой	other(s)	материал	material
жизнь	life	менее	less
заведение	institution, establishment	меньший	smaller
		место	place, situation

78

мир	peace; world	предмет	article, object; subject, topic
много	much, many	проблема	problem
мысль	thought	прочий	other
некоторый	some, certain	путь	way, path, journey
несколько	several, a few, some	разный	various, different
новый	new	ранний	early
область	province, region; sphere	роль	role, part
общественный	public, social	самый	most; the very ...; same
основной	basic, fundamental	свет	world; light
отдельный	separate, detached	связь	connection, link; communications
отношение	relation(ship), attitude; (in pl.) relations	середина	middle
отрасль	branch, field, special sphere (of work, knowledge)	система	system
		следовать	(ipfve) to follow
		следующий	following
		смешанный	mixed
полный	full	средний	middle (adj.)
положение	position; standing, situation; regulations	старый	old, ancient
		указать	to show
		характер	character, nature
получать	(ipfve), получить (pfve) to receive	целый	whole, full
		центральный	central
последний	last, latest	часть	part, section
правда	truth	человек	person, man

3. *Abbreviations* (for expansions see full list in 7.3)

авт.	author	бел.	Belorussian
аз(ер).	Azerbaidzhani	беспл.	free of charge
А(з)ССР	Azerbaidzhani SSR	б-ка	library
АН	Academy of Sciences	БСЭ	Great Soviet Encylopedia
арм.	Armenian		
Арм ССР	Armenian SSR	БССР	Belorussian SSR

б.ц.	unpriced	ин-т	institute
в.	century, age, era	ист.	historic(al)
вв.	centuries	и т.д.	and so on, etc.
вкл.	inclusive (adv.)	ИХЛ	'Literature' Publishing House
ВКП(б)	All-Union Communist Party (Bolsheviks) [1925–52]	к.	kopek(s)
		каз.	Kazakh
вып.	issue	К(аз)ССР	Kazakh SSR
г.	year; town	кир(г).	Kirghiz
ГАУ	Chief Directorate of Archives	кн.	book
		кн-во	publishing house
гг.	years	КПСС	Communist Party of the Soviet Union
ГДР	German Democratic Republic		
		л.	printers' sheet
ГИХЛ	State Publishing House for Literature	Л.	Leningrad
		лат.	Latvian
гл.	chapter; main, chief	Латв ССР	Latvian SSR
гос.	state (adj.)	ЛГУ	Leningrad State University
госуд.	state (adj.)		
груз.	Georgian	лит.	Lithuanian
Г(руз)ССР	Georgian SSR	Лит ССР	Lithuanian SSR
ГУГК	Chief Directorate of Geodesy and Cartography	М.	Moscow
		м-во	ministry
		МГУ	Moscow State University
ДАН	Reports of the Academy of Sciences		
		Мол. гв.	'Young Guard' Publishing House
доп.	supplement (-ed)	молд.	Moldavian
др.	other(s)	МССР	Moldavian SSR
изд.	edition; impression, publication	назв.	name, title
		напр.	for example, *eg*
изд-во	publishing house	нар.	peoples', popular, national
илл.	illustration(s)		
им.	named (after)	нем.	German
ИМО	'International Relations' Publishing House	НОТ	scientific organisation of labour, 'O & M'
		н.э.	A.D.

80

о-во	society; company	сокр.	abbreviation, abbreviated
ОГИЗ	Union of State Publishing Houses [1930–49]	сост.	compiler; compiled by
ООН	UNO	соч.	work, composition
отв.	responsible, in charge	Спб.	St. Petersburg
		ср.	compare, cf.
отд.	section, department; separate, detached	СССР	Union of Soviet Socialist Republics
п	first impression	стол.	century
П.	Petrograd	стр.	page
пер.	binding, hard cover; translation; street	США	USA
		т.	volume
поз.	item number	тадж.	Tadzhik
прим(еч).	note, comment	Тадж ССР	Ṭadzhik SSR
проч.	other	т.е.	that is, *ie*
р.	rouble(s)	тип.	printing house
ред.	editor; editorial; editorship	тит. л.	title-page
		т.н.	so-called
РЖ	'Abstracts Journal'	тр.	transactions
рис.	drawing	ТССР	Turkmenian SSR
РКП(б)	Russian Communist Party (Bolsheviks) [1919–25]	тт.	volumes
		туркм.	Turkmenian
		тыс.	thousand
РСДРП(б)	Russian Social-Democratic Workers' Party (Bolsheviks) [1898–1918]	узб.	Uzbek
		Уз(б) ССР	Uzbek SSR
		укр.	Ukrainian
		ул.	street
РСФСР	Russian Soviet Federal Socialist Republic	ун-т	university
		УССР	Ukrainian SSR
		фр.	French
рус.	Russian	ФРГ	Federal Republic of Germany
с.	page		
см.	see, refer to; centimetre	ц.	price
		ЦК	Central Committee
собр.	collection	ч.	part, section

черт.	drawing	экз.	copy, specimen
ЭВМ	computer		

4. Scholarship and culture

академия	academy	сравнитель-	comparative
архив	archives	ный	
библиотека	library	театр	theatre
заведение	institution, establish- ment	учёный	learned, scholarly, academic, scientific
кино	cinema	филиал	branch
культура	culture	фонд	stock; (in library) holdings, collection
музей	museum		
наука	science, scholarship	художествен-	artistic, to do with
научный	scientific, scholarly, academic	ный	the arts
		член	member
памятник	monument, relic		

5. Writing and authorship

автор	author	произведе-	work, production
журна- листика	journalism	ние	
		прочитать	(pfve) to read
книга	book	рукопись	manuscript
книжный	book (adj.), bookish	составитель	compiler, writer
написать	(pfve) to write	составить	(pfve) to compile
перевод	translation	сотрудник	collaborator
писатель	writer	сочинение	work, composition
писать	(ipfve) to write	творчество	creation, creative work
подгото- вить	(pfve) to prepare		
		читатель	reader
подготовлен- ный	prepared	читать	(ipfve) to read

6. Types of publication

авторефе- рат	synopsis of thesis	альманах	anthology, literary miscellany
альбом	album, volume of illustrations	библиогра- фия	bibliography

биография	biography	календарь	calendar
брошюра	booklet, pamphlet	карта	map; card
буклет	(illustrated) booklet, pamphlet	картина	picture, painting
		комплект	(complete) set, full number
бюллетень	bulletin		
ведомость	list, register. (pl.) record, gazette	летопись	chronicle, annals
		литература	literature (not necessarily fiction)
вестник	messenger; bulletin		
воспоминание	memory. (pl.) memoirs	непериодический	irregular (of a periodical, series)
выпуск	issue	номер	number, issue
газета	newspaper	ноты	(pl.) (sheet) music
дневник	diary	обзор	survey, review
доклад	report, address, paper, lecture	обозрение	review
		описание	description
дополнение	supplement	отдельный	separate, detached
ежегодник	annual	открытка	postcard
ежемесячник	monthly	отчёт	account, report
		оттиск	offprint, reprint; impression
еженедельник	weekly		
		очерк	sketch, essay, outline
жизнеописание	biography		
		перепечатка	reprint
журнал	periodical, journal	переписка	correspondence
записка	note, (pl.) notes, transactions	перечень	list
		периодический	periodical (adj.)
запись	record, entry; recording, booking		
		письмо	letter
избранный	selected	плакат	poster, wall sheet
известия	(pl.) news; transactions	повесть	tale, story
		полутом	half-volume
издание	edition; impression; publication	пособие	text-book
		поэзия	poetry
информация	information	продолжающийся	continuing, serial
исследование	investigation, research		

83

продолже-ние	continuation	серия	serial
проза	prose	сказание	story, legend
проспект	prospectus	сказка	tale, story
публици-стика	essay-writing (esp. on social and political matters); journalism	словарь	dictionary
		собрание	collection; gathering, meeting
путеводи-тель	guide (-book)	совещание	conference, meeting
		сообщение	report, information, communication
пьеса	play	справочник	handbook, guide
разговор-ник	phrase-book	стандарт	standard (noun)
		статья	article
рассказ	story, tale	стих	verse (pl.) poetry
репродук-ция	reproduction	стихотворе-ние	poem
реферат	abstract; paper, essay	тетрадь	writing-book, copy-book; fascicule, part (of contin-uation)
рецензия	review		
роман	novel		
сборник	collection, symposium, volume of articles	труд	labour; (pl.) transactions
сведение	information. (pl.) particulars	учебник	textbook, manual
		хрестоматия	collection of readings
сводный	combined; summary (adj.)	энциклопе-дия	encyclopedia
серийный	serial (adj.)		

7. The book: physical characteristics

бумага	paper	заключение	conclusion
введение	introduction	заметка	note, notice
вступитель-ный	introductory, opening	изменение	alteration
		иллюстра-ция	illustration
глава	chapter; head, chief (noun)	исправление	correction
заглавие	title, heading	конец	end, finish

краска	paint; (pl.) colour(s)	предисловие	preface, foreword
лист	leaf; sheet of paper (esp. printers' sheet, usually equivalent to 16 printed pages)	приложение	appendix, supplement
		примечание	note, comment
		резюме	summary (often in another language)
название	name, title	рисунок	drawing
начало	beginning	содержание	contents
обложка	paper cover	стереотип-	stereotype(d)
оборот	back, verso	ный	
оглавление	table of contents	страница	page
опечатка	misprint, erratum	таблица	table; plate (in book)
переплёт	binding, hard cover		
печатный	printed	том	volume
поправка	correction	титульный	title-page
посвящение	dedication	лист	
послесловие	postscript, afterword	чертёж	drawing, draft

8. Publishing and bookselling

бесплатно	free of charge	опублико-	(pfve) to publish; (-ся) to be published
выйти	(pfve), выходить (ipfve) to go out; appear, be published	вать	
		переимено-	renamed
заявка	order, claim	занный	
издавать	(ipfve), издать (pfve) to publish	печать	press; printing; seal, stamp
издатель- ство	publishing house	повторно	again
		прекращён-	ceased, discontinued
книгоизда- тельство	publishing house	ный	
		публиковать	(ipfve) to publish. (-ся) to be published
книготорго- вля	book-trade		
неизданный	unpublished	редкий	rare
объявлен- ный	announced	редактор	editor
		редакцион- ный	editorial (adj.)

редакция	editorial staff; editorship	типография	printing house
редколлегия	editorial board	тираж	size of edition, number of copies

9. *Publishing houses in the USSR*

This select list includes only publishers in Moscow and Leningrad (*ie* only the major publishers in the Russian language) and only those currently (1972) in existence. Subject range is given where not evident from the title.

'Аврора'	'Aurora'. (Art books for export)
АПН	'News' Press Agency. (Books on many aspects of Soviet life, primarily for readers abroad)
Атомиздат	(Science and technology of atomic energy)
Воениздат	(Contemporary and historical military and naval topics)
'Высшая школа'	'Higher School'. (Textbooks and other instructional matter for university and other higher education courses)
Гидрометеоиздат	(Meteorology, hydrology, oceanography)
'Детская литература'	'Childrens' Literature'
Издательство Ленинградского госуниверситета	Publishing House of Leningrad State University. (Scholarly works in most subjects)
Издательство Московского госуниверситета	Publishing House of Moscow State University. (Scholarly works in most subjects)
Издательство стандартов	Publishing House for Standards. (Industrial and other standards and associated literature)
'Искусство'	'Art'. (Theatre, cinema, fine arts)
'Книга'	'Book'. (Publishing, printing, bibliography and librarianship)
'Колос'	'Ear of Corn' [!] (Agriculture)
'Лёгкая индустрия'	'Light Industry'. (Textile, garment and service industries)
'Лесная промышленность'	'Timber Industry'

'Машиностроение'	'Mechanical Engineering'
'Медицина'	'Medicine'
'Международные отношения'	'International Relations'. (International policy, trade and law; material for learners of languages spoken outside the USSR)
'Металлургия'	'Metallurgy'. (Metal industry, metallurgy)
'Молодая гвардия'	'Young Guard'. (Publishing organ of the Komsomol. Political, literary and informational books for young people)
'Московский рабочий'	'Moscow Worker'. (Large-circulation popular works)
'Музыка'	'Music'
'Мысль'	'Thought'. (Economics, philosophy, history and Marxism-Leninism)
'Наука'	'Science'. (Scholarly works on all subjects. Publisher for the Academy of Sciences of the USSR)
'Недра'	'The Earth'. (Geology, geophysics, geodesy)
'Педагогика'	'Pedagogics'. (Educational theory and practice)
Политиздат	(Marxist-Leninist classics, Party and Soviet history, Party organisation, mass-circulation political literature)
'Прогресс'	'Progress'. (Translations into non-Soviet languages of a wide range of Soviet publications, and into Russian of foreign works)
'Просвещение'	'Education'. (Textbooks and other instructional matter for general and special schools)
Профиздат	(Trade unions, 'socialist competition')
'Связь'	'Communications'. (Radio and television, postal services and telecommunications)
'Советская энциклопедия'	'Soviet Encyclopedia'. (Encyclopedias and dictionaries)

'Советский композитор'	'Soviet Composer'. (Scores and musical literature)
'Советский писатель'	'Soviet Writer'. (Publisher for the Writers' Union of the USSR. Soviet imaginative literature and literary studies)
'Статистика'	'Statistics'
Стройиздат	(Construction, architecture and town planning)
'Транспорт'	'Transport'
'Физкультура и спорт'	'Physical Culture and Sport'
'Финансы'	'Finance'
'Химия'	'Chemistry'. (Chemistry and chemical technology)
'Художественная литература'	'Literature'. (Soviet and classical Russian literature, Russian translations of foreign literature, literary studies)
'Экономика'	'Economics'
'Энергия'	'Energy'. (Power production, its technology and industries)
'Юридическая литература'	'Legal literature'

10. Bibliographical and reference work

алфавитный	alphabetical
аннотированный	annotated
библиографический	bibliographical
библиография	bibliography
вспомогательный	auxiliary, subsidiary
именной	name (adj.). именной указатель name index
предметный	subject (adj.). предметный указатель subject index
рекомендательный	recommendatory, recommended
сводный	combined. сводный каталог union catalogue
список	list

| ссылка | reference; exile, banishment |
| указатель | index |

11. Education

воспитание	upbringing, training, education
вуз	higher educational institution
курс	course
педагогика	pedagogics, education
преподавание	teaching, instruction
просвещение	education, enlightenment
студент	student
университет	university
урок	lesson
учебный	educational, training (adj.)
учение	studies
учитель	teacher
школа	school. высшая школа : higher school (*ie* university)

12. Politics and administration

большевик	Bolshevik	гражданский	civic, civil
буржуазный	'bourgeois'	движение	movement
верховный	supreme. Верховный Совет Supreme Soviet	закон	law
		заместитель	deputy
		зарубежный	foreign
		заседание	session, sitting
внешний	external, outward	иностранец	foreigner
внутренний	internal, inward	иностран- ный	foreign
война	war		
вооружён- ный	armed. вооружён- ные силы armed forces	коллегия	board, committee
		комсомол	Komsomol, Young Communist League
восстание	uprising, revolt	коллектив	collective
всесоюзный	all-Union	комитет	committee
государст- венный	state (adj.)	коммунисти- ческий	Communist (adj.)

красный	red
крестьянин	(pl. крестьяне) peasant
международ-ный	international
министер-ство	ministry
народ	people, nation
националь-ный	national, of nationalities (esp. of non-Russian minorities in the USSR)
область	province, region; sphere
общество	society; company
отдел	section, department
партийный	Party (adj. — normally of the Communist Party)
партия	(political) party. (in the USSR usually the Communist Party)
пленум	plenum, full meeting
право	right(s); law
председа-тель	chairman
профсоюз	trade union
революция	revolution
республика	republic
речь	speech
решение	resolution, declaration
сессия	session
совещание	conference, meeting
совет	soviet, council
Советский Союз	Soviet Union
созыв	convocation (*eg* of the Supreme Soviet)
союз	union
съезд	congress
управление	administration, directorate
устав	statutes, regulations, charter
юридиче-ский	legal, juridical

13. Economics and planning

колхоз	collective farm
копейка	kopek (1/100 of a rouble)
население	population
планиро-вание	planning
производ-ство	production, manufacture
промыш-ленность	industry
пятилетка	five-year plan
работа	work, activity
рабочий	working; worker
развивать	(ipfve), развить (pfve) to develop. (-ся)to develop, be developed

развитие	development	учёт	accounting
рубль	rouble	финансы	finance
сельское хозяйство	agriculture	фунт	pound (Sterling)
сельскохоз- яйственный	agricultural	хозяйство	economy; sector of the economy
		цена	price
совхоз	sovkhoz, State farm	цифра	figure
статистика	statistics	экономика	economics, economic structure
стоимость	cost, price, value		
торговля	trade, commerce	экономия	economy
трудящийся	worker (declined as adj.)		

14. History

Декабрист	Decembrist, partici-pant in the St. Petersburg revolt, December 1825	Иван Грозный	Tsar Ivan IV (the Terrible), 1530–84
		историче-ский	historic(al)
дооктябрь-ский	pre-October (*ie* before the October Revolution of 1917)	историк	historian
		история	history
		источник	source
дореволю-ционный	pre-Revolutionary (*ie* before the October Revolution)	князь	prince
		кремль	fortress, Kremlin (not only in Moscow)
древний	ancient	летопись	chronicle, annals
Екатерина II	Empress Catherine II (the Great), 1729–96	Пётр Великий	Tsar Peter I (the Great), 1672–1725
		царь	tsar

15. The arts

живопись	painting	изобрази-тельный	figurative, illustrative. изобразительное искусство fine, figurative art(s)

искусство	art	художест-	artistic, to do with
музыка	music	венный	the arts (in the
музыкаль-	musical		broad sense)
ный		художник	artist, designer
творчество	creation, creative		
	work		

16. Literature and language

грамматика	grammar	речь	speech
драматургия	the drama, play-	слово	word
	writing	стиль	style
литература	literature (not	филология	philology; literary
	necessarily fiction)		and linguistic
литератур-	literary		studies
ный		фольклор	folklore
литературо-	history of literature,	язык	language
ведение	literary studies	языкознание	linguistics
поэт	poet		

17. Science and technology

вычислитель-	computing (adj.)	прикладной	applied
ный		природа	nature
горное дело	mining	связь	connection, link;
естествен-	natural. естествен-		communications
ный	ные науки the	строитель-	building, construction
	natural sciences	ство	(also in figurative
итог	sum, total, result		sense)
математика	mathematics	техника	technology;
медицина	medicine		technique
металлургия	metallurgy, metal	физика	physics
	industry	химия	chemistry
наука	science, scholarship	энергетика	power (production
научный	scientific, scholarly,		and industry)
	academic		
опыт	trial, experiment,		
	attempt		

18. Personal and social life

город	(pl. города) town	рождение	birth
дети	children	семья	family
дом	house	социальный	social
молодёжь	youth, young people	улица	street
почта	post	церковь	church

19. Time

век	(pl. века) century, age, era	еженедель-ный	weekly (adj.)
впервые	for the first time	квартал	quarter (esp. of a year)
время	(gen. sg. времени, nom. pl. времена, gen. pl. времён) time	лета	(gen. pl. лет) years
		месяц	month
		настоящий	present, current
год	year. в году in the year	неделя	week
		современ-ный	contemporary
день	(pl. дни) day		
ежегодный	annual (adj.)	столетие	century
ежемесяч-ный	monthly (adj.)	эпоха	epoch, age
		эра	era

20. Months of the year
(in calendar order)

январь	January	июль	July
февраль	February	август	August
март	March	сентябрь	September
апрель	April	октябрь	October
май	May	ноябрь	November
июнь	June	декабрь	December

21. Geographical terms (except USSR)

Азия	Asia	Великобри-тания	Great Britain
английский	English		
Англия	England	венгерский	Hungarian

Венгрия	Hungary	море	sea
восток	east	Мюнхен	Munich
восточный	eastern	Нью-Йорк	New York
Гаага	The Hague	Париж	Paris
Германия	Germany	польский	Polish
Греция	Greece	Польша	Poland
греческий	Greek	район	region, district, area
Дальний Восток	Far East	Рим	Rome
еврей	Jew	рубеж	border, boundary.
еврейский	Jewish; (of language) Yiddish		за рубежом abroad
Европа	Europe	север	north
европей- ский	European	северный	northern
запад	west	славянский	Slavonic, Slavic
западный	western	словацкий	Slovak
зарубежный	foreign	страна	country, land
Испания	Spain	турецкий	Turkish
испанский	Spanish	Турция	Turkey
Китай	China	Франция	France
китайский	Chinese	французский	French
		чешский	Czech
		юг	south
		южный	southern

22. Geographical terms (USSR)

азербайджанский	Azerbaidzhani
Алма-Ата	Alma-Ata (capital of the Kazakh SSR)
Армения	Armenia
армянский	Armenian
Ашхабад	Ashkhabad (capital of the Turkmen SSR)
Баку	Baku (capital of the Azerbaidzhani SSR)
Белороссия	Belorussia, White Russia
белорусский	Belorussian
Вильнюс	Vilnius (capital of the Lithuanian SSR)
грузинский	Georgian
Грузия	Georgia
Душанбе	Dushanbe (capital of the Tadzhik SSR)

94

Ереван	Erevan (capital of the Armenian SSR)
Закавказье	the Transcaucasus
Кавказ	the Caucasus
казахский	Kazakh (adj.)
Карпаты	the Carpathians
Киев	Kiev (capital of the Ukrainian SSR)
киргизский	Kirghiz (adj.)
Кишинёв	Kishinev (capital of the Moldavian SSR)
Крым	the Crimea
латвийский	Latvian
Ленинград	Leningrad (to 1914 St. Petersburg, 1914–24 Petrograd)
Литва	Lithuania
Минск	Minsk (capital of the Belorussian SSR)
молдавский	Moldavian
Москва	Moscow
московский	Moscow (adj.), Muscovite
Петроград	Petrograd (1914–24. Formerly St. Petersburg, then Leningrad)
Поволжье	the Volga region
Рига	Riga (capital of the Latvian SSR)
Россия	Russia
российский	Russian (applied especially to the pre-1917 Russian empire)
русский	Russian (applied to the Russian language and people)
Русь	Rus', (ancient) Russia
Санктпетербург	St. Petersburg (to 1914, then Petrograd, then Leningrad)
Сибирь	Siberia
Советский Союз	Soviet Union
таджикский	Tadzhik (adj.)
Таллин	Tallinn (capital of the Estonian SSR)
Ташкент	Tashkent (capital of the Uzbek SSR)
Тбилиси	Tbilisi, Tiflis (capital of the Georgian SSR)
туркменский	Turkmen (adj.)

узбекский	Uzbek (adj.)
Украина	the Ukraine
украинский	Ukrainian
Урал	the Urals
Фрунзе	Frunze (capital of the Kirghiz SSR)
Чёрное море	the Black Sea
эстонский	Estonian

7.3. COMPLETE VOCABULARY

a	and, but
август	August
'Аврора'	'Aurora' publishing house (see 7.2.9)
авт. (= автор)	author
автор	author
автореферат	synopsis of thesis (prepared by candidate)
аз(ер). (= азербайджанский)	Azerbaidzhani (adj.)
азербайджанский	Azerbaidzhani (adj.)
Азия	Asia
А(з)ССР	Azerbaidzhani SSR
академия	academy
алфавитный	alphabetical
альбом	album, volume of illustrations
Алма-Ата	Alma-Ata (capital of the Kazakh SSR)
альманах	anthology, literary miscellany
АН (= Академия Наук)	Academy of Sciences
англ. (= английский)	English
английский	English
Англия	England
аннотированный	annotated
АПН (= Агентство печати 'Новости')	'Novosti' Press Agency (see 7.2.9)
апрель	April
арм. (= армянский)	Armenian
Армения	Armenia
Арм ССР	Armenian SSR

армянский	Armenian
архив	archives
АССР (=автономная советская социалистическая республика)	Autonomous Soviet Socialist Republic
Атомиздат	[publishing house — see 7.2.9]
Ашхабад	Ashkhabad (capital of the Turkmen SSR)
Баку	Baku (capital of the Azerbaidzhani SSR)
без	(with gen.) without
бел. (= белорусский)	Belorussian
Белороссия	Belorussia, White Russia
белорусский	Belorussian
белый	white
беспл. (= бесплатно)	free of charge
бесплатно	free of charge
библиографический	bibliographical
библиография	bibliography
библиотека	library
библиотечный	library (adj.)
биографический	biographical
биография	biography
б-ка (= библиотека)	library
более	more
большевик	Bolshevik
большой	great, big
брошюра	booklet, pamphlet
БСЭ (= Большая Советская Энциклопедия)	Great Soviet Encyclopedia
БССР	Belorussian SSR
будущий	future, next
буклет	(illustrated) booklet, pamphlet
бумага	paper
буржуазный	'bourgeois'
б.ц. (= без цены)	unpriced
быть	to be
бюллетень	bulletin

в	(with acc.) into, at, (with loc.) in, at
в. (= век)	century, age, era
важный	important
ваш	your, yours
вв. (= века)	centuries
введение	introduction
ведомость	list, register; (pl.) record, gazette
век (pl. века)	century, age, era
Великая Октябрьская социалистическая революция	Great October Socialist Revolution (of 1917)
Великая Отечественная Война	Great Patriotic War (1941–45)
великий	great
Великобритания	Great Britain
венгерский	Hungarian
Венгрия	Hungary
вестник	bulletin; messenger
весь, вся, всё, все	all
верховный	supreme. Верховный Совет Supreme Soviet
Вильнюс	Vilnius (capital of the Lithuanian SSR)
вкл. (= включительно)	inclusive
включать	(ipfve), включить (pfve) to contain
включительно	inclusive (adv.)
ВКП(б) (= Всесоюзная коммунистическая партия (большевиков))	All-Union Communist Party (Bolsheviks) (title of the Communist Party of the Soviet Union, 1925–52)
вместо	(with gen.) instead of
внешний	external, outward
внимание	attention
внутренний	internal, inward
во	[variant of в]
Воениздат	[publishing house – see 7.2.9]
военный	military, war-
война	war
вооружённый	armed. вооружённые силы armed forces

98

вопрос	question, matter
восемнадцать	eighteen
восемь	eight
восемьдесят	eighty
воспитание	upbringing, training, education
воспоминание	memory; (pl.) memoirs
восстание	uprising, revolt
восток	east
восточный	eastern
восьмой	eighth
впервые	for the first time
время	(gen. sing. времени, nom. pl. времена, gen. pl. времён) time
все, вся	all
всеобщий	universal, general
всесоюзный	all-Union
вспомогательный	auxiliary, subsidiary
вступительный	introductory, opening
второй	second (=2nd)
вуз (= высшее учебное заведение)	higher educational institution
вы	you
выдающийся	prominent, distinguished
выйти	(pfve) to go out, appear, be published
вып. (= выпуск)	issue
выпуск	issue
высокий	high
'Высшая школа'	'Higher School' (*ie* 'University') publishing house (see 7.2.9)
высший	higher
выходить	(ipfve) to go out, appear, be published
вычислительный	computing (adj.)
г. (= год)	year
(= город)	town
Гаага	The Hague

газета	newspaper
ГАУ (= Главное архивное управление)	Chief Directorate of Archives
гг. (= годы)	years
где	where
ГДР	German Democratic Republic (East Germany)
Германия	Germany
Гидрометеоиздат	[publishing house – see 7.2.9]
ГИХЛ (= Госуд. изд-во художественной литературы)	State Publishing House for Literature
гл. (= глава)	chapter
(= главный)	main, chief (adj.)
глава	chapter; head, chief (noun)
главный	main, principal, head, chief (adj.)
год	year. в году in the year
горное дело	mining
город (pl. города)	town
гос. (= государственный)	state (adj.)
Госиздат (= Государственное издательство)	State Publishing House
Гослитиздат (= Госуд. изд-во художественной литературы	State Publishing House for Literature
Госполитиздат (= Госуд. изд-во политической литературы)	State Publishing House for Political Literature
госуд. (= государственный)	state (adj.)
государственный	state (adj.)
государство	state (noun)
Госюриздат (= Госуд. изд-во юридической литературы)	State Publishing House for Legal Literature
готовить	(ipfve) to prepare. (-ся) to be prepared
гражданский	civic, civil
грамматика	grammar
Греция	Greece
греческий	Greek
груз. (= грузинский)	Georgian

грузинский	Georgian
Грузия	Georgia
Г(руз) ССР	Georgian SSR
ГУГК (= Главное управление геодезии и картографии)	Chief Directorate of Geodesy and Cartography
дальний	distant. Дальний Восток Far East
ДАН (= Доклады Академии Наук)	Reports of the Academy of Sciences
два, две	two
двадцать	twenty
двенадцать	twelve
двести	two hundred
движение	movement
девяносто	ninety
девятнадцать	nineteen
девятый	ninth
девять	nine
декабрист	Decembrist, participant in the St. Petersburg revolt of December 1825
декабрь	December
дело	affair, matter, business
день	day
десятый	tenth
десять	ten
Детгиз	State Publishing House for Childrens' Literature
дети	children
'Детская литература'	'Childrens' Literature' publishing house
детский	childrens'
деятель	functionary, worker; person, figure
для	(with gen.) for
дневник	diary
дни	(nom. pl.) days
до	(with gen.) until, up to
доклад	report, address, paper, lecture

должно быть	should be
дом	house
до н.э. (= до нашей эры)	B.C.
дооктябрьский	pre-October (*ie* before the 1917 October Revolution)
доп. (= дополнение, дополненный)	supplement, supplemented
дополнение	supplement
дополненный	supplemented
дополнительный	supplementary
дореволюционный	pre-Revolutionary (*ie* before the October Revolution)
др. (= другой)	other(s)
драматургия	the drama, playwriting
древний	ancient
другой	other(s)
Душанбе	Dushanbe (capital of the Tadzhik SSR)
еврей	Jew
еврейский	Jewish; (of language) Yiddish
Европа	Europe
европейский	European
его	him, it; his, its
ежегодник	annual (noun)
ежегодный	annual (adj.)
ежемесячник	monthly (noun)
ежемесячный	monthly (adj.)
еженедельник	weekly (noun)
еженедельный	weekly (adj.)
её	her, hers; it, its
Екатерина II	Empress Catherine II (the Great), 1729–96
Ереван	Erevan (capital of the Armenian SSR)
естественный	natural
ещё	still, yet

живопись	painting
жизнеописание	biography
жизнь	life
журнал	periodical, journal
журналистика	journalism
за	(with acc.) for; during; behind. (with instr.) for; owing to; behind
заведение	institution, establishment
заглавие	title, heading
заготовка	state purchases; (in pl.) procurement, supply
задача	problem, task, object
Закавказье	Transcaucasia
заключение	conclusion
закон	law
заместитель	deputy
заметка	note, notice
запад	west
западный	western
записка	note; (pl.) notes; transactions
запись	record, entry; recording, booking
зарубежный	foreign
заседание	session, sitting
заявка	order, claim
здравоохранение	public health
значение	meaning, significance
и	and, also
Иван Грозный	Tsar Ivan IV (the Terrible), 1530–84
и др. (= и другие)	and others, *et al.*
из	(with gen.) from, out of
избранный	selected
известия	news; transactions
изд. (= издание)	edition; impression; publication
(= издательство)	publishing house

издавать	(ipfve), издать (pfve) to publish. (-ся) to be published
издание	edition; impression; publication
издательство	publishing house
изд-во (= издательство)	publishing house
изменение	alteration
изобразительный	figurative, illustrative
или	or
илл. (= иллюстрация)	illustration
иллюстрация	illustration
им. (= имени)	named after (with gen.)
имени	named after (with gen.)
именной	name (adj.). именной указатель name index
ИМО	'International Relations' Publishing House (see 7.2.9)
иностранец	foreigner
иностранный	foreign
ин-т (= институт)	institute
информация	information
искусство	art
'Искусство'	'Art' Publishing House (see 7.2.9)
Испания	Spain
испанский	Spanish
исправление	correction
исследование	investigation, research
ист. (= исторический)	historic(al)
историк	historian
исторический	historic(al)
история	history
источник	source
и т.д. (= и так далее)	and so on, etc.
итог	sum, total, result
их	of them, their, theirs
ИХЛ (= Изд-во 'Художественная литература')	'Literature' Publishing House

104

июль	July
июнь	June
к	(with dat.) to, up to, towards
к. (= копейка)	kopek (1/100 of a rouble)
Кавказ	Caucasus
каз. (= казахский)	Kazakh (adj.)
К(аз) ССР	Kazakh SSR
как	how
календарь	calendar
Карпаты	Carpathians
карта	map; card
картина	picture, painting
картографический	cartographic, map (adj.)
квартал	quarter (esp. of year)
Киев	Kiev (capital of the Ukrainian SSR)
кино	cinema
кир(г). (= киргизский)	Kirghiz (adj.)
киргизский	Kirghiz (adj.)
Китай	China
китайский	Chinese
Кишинёв	Kishinëv (capital of Moldavian SSR)
кн. (= книга)	book
кн-во (= книгоиздательство)	publishing house
книга	book
'Книга'	'Book' Publishing House (see 7.2.9)
книговедение	study of books, bibliology
книгоиздательство	publishing house
книготорговля	book-trade
книжный	book (adj.), bookish
князь	prince
ко	(variant of к) (with dat.) to, up to, towards
коллегия	board, committee
коллектив	collective, group

'Колос'	'Ear of Corn' Publishing House (see 7.2.9)
колхоз	collective farm
коммунальный	communal, municipal, local
коммунистический	Communist (adj.)
комплект	(complete) set; full number
конец	end, finish
кончать	(ipfve), кончить (pfve) to finish, end. (-ся) to be finished, ended
копейка	kopek (1/100 of a rouble)
КПСС (= Коммунистическая партия Советского Союза)	Communist Party of the Soviet Union
краска	paint; (in pl.) colour(s)
красный	red
краткий	short
кремль	fortress, Kremlin (not only in Moscow)
крестьянин	(pl. крестьяне) peasant
кроме	(with gen.) besides, except
Крым	the Crimea
кто	who
культура	culture
курс	course
л. (= лист)	leaf; sheet of paper, printers' sheet (usually equal to 16 numbered pages)
Л. (= Ленинград)	Leningrad
лат. (=латвийский, латышский)	Latvian, Lettish
латвийский	Latvian, Lettish
Латв ССР	Latvian SSR
латышский	Latvian, Lettish
ЛГУ (= Ленинградский госуд. ун-т)	Leningrad State University
'Лёгкая индустрия'	'Light Industry' Publishing House (see 7.2.9)
лёгкий	light

Лениздат	Periodical and Book Publishing House of the Leningrad District and City Committees of the CPSU
Ленинград	Leningrad (formerly St. Petersburg and Petrograd)
'Лесная промышленность'	'Timber Industry' Publishing House
лета	(gen. pl. лет) years
летопись	chronicle, annals
лист	leaf; sheet of paper, printers' sheet (usually equal to 16 pages)
лит. (= литовский)	Lithuanian
Литва	Lithuania
литература	literature (not necessarily fiction)
литературный	literary
литературоведение	history of literature, literary criticism
литовский	Lithuanian
Лит ССР	Lithuanian SSR
лучший	better, best
люди	people
М. (= Москва)	Moscow
май	May
март	March
материал	material
машиностроение	mechanical engineering, engineering industry
'Машиностроение'	'Mechanical Engineering' Publishing House
математика	mathematics
м-во (= министерство)	ministry
МГУ (= Московский госуд. ун-т)	Moscow State University
медицина	medicine
'Медицина'	'Medicine' Publishing House
между	(with instr.) between, among
международный	international

'Международные отношения'	'International Relations' Publishing House (see 7.2.9)
менее	less
меньший	smaller
место	place, situation
месяц	month
металлургия	metallurgy, metal industry
'Металлургия'	'Metallurgy' Publishing House (see 7.2.9)
министерство	ministry
Минск	Minsk (capital of the Belorussian SSR)
мир	peace; world
много	much, many
мой, моя, моё, мои	my, mine
Мол. гв. (= 'Молодая гвардия')	'Young Guard' Publishing House (see 7.2.9)
молд. (= молдавский)	Moldavian
молдавский	Moldavian
'Молодая гвардия'	'Young Guard' Publishing House (see 7.2.9)
молодёжь	youth, young people
море	sea
Москва	Moscow
московский	Moscow (adj.), Muscovite
МССР	Moldavian SSR
Музгиз (= Госуд. музыкаль- ное изд-во)	State Musical Publishing House
музей	museum
музыка	music
'Музыка'	'Music' Publishing House
музыкальный	musical
мы	we
мысль	thought
'Мысль'	'Thought' Publishing House (see 7.2.9)
Мюнхен	Munich
на	(with acc.) on to ⎱ and many other mean- (with loc.) on ⎰ ings in set phrases

108

над	(with instr.) over, above
назв. (= название)	name, title
название	name, title
написать	(pfve) to write
напр. (= например)	for example, *eg*
нар. (= народный)	peoples', popular, national
народ	people, nation
народный	peoples', popular, national
население	population
настоящий	present, current
наука	science, scholarship
'Наука'	'Science' Publishing House (see 7.2.9)
научный	scientific, scholarly, academic
национальный	national, of nationalities (esp. of non-Russian minorities in the USSR)
начало	beginning
наш	our, ours
не	not
неделя	week
'Недра'	'The Earth' Publishing House (see 7.2.9)
неизданный	unpublished
некоторый	some, certain
нем. (= немецкий)	German
немецкий	German
непериодический	irregular (of a journal, series)
несколько	several, a few
но	but
новый	new
номер	number; issue
НОТ (= научная организация труда)	scientific organisation of labour, 'organisation and methods' work
нота	musical note; (pl.) music
нотный	musical
ноябрь	November
Нью-Йорк	New York
н.э. (= нашей эры)	A.D.

о, об	(with acc.) against, along
	(with loc.) about, concerning, on
обзор	survey, review
область	province, region; sphere
обложка	paper cover
обозрение	review
оборот	back, verso
обслуживание	service; facilities
общественный	public, social
общество	society; company
общий	general, common; total
объём	size, amount
объявленный	announced
о-во (= общество)	society; company
ОГИЗ (= Объединение госуд. издательств)	Union of State Publishing Houses (1930–1949)
оглавление	table of contents
один, одна, одно	one
одиннадцать	eleven
около	(with gen.) about, around
октябрь	October
он, она, оно	he, she, it
они	they
ООН	UNO
опечатка	misprint, erratum
описание	description
опубликовать	(pfve) to publish. (-ся) to be published
опыт	trial, experiment, attempt
организация	organisation
основа	basis, fundamental (noun)
основной	basic, fundamental (adj.)
особенно	especially
от	(with gen.) from, away from
отв. (= ответственный)	responsible, in charge
ответственный	responsible, in charge

отд. (= отдел(ение))	section, department
(= отдельный)	separate, detached
отдел(ение)	section, department
отдельный	separate, detached
открытка	postcard
отношение	attitude, relation(ship); (pl.) relations
отрасль	branch, field, special sphere
оттиск	offprint; reprint; impression
отчёт	account, report
очерк	sketch, outline, essay
п	first impression (abbrev. in *Knizhnaya letopis'*)
П. (= Петроград)	Petrograd (until 1914 St. Petersburg, from 1924 Leningrad)
памятник	monument, relic
Париж	Paris
партийный	Party (adj.)
партия	(political) party (in the USSR usually the Communist Party of the Soviet Union)
педагогика	pedagogics, education
'Педагогика'	'Pedagogics' Publishing House (see 7.2.9)
пер. (= перевод)	translation
(= переплёт)	binding, hard cover
(= переулок)	street (in town), lane, alley
первый	first
перевод	translation
переименованный	re-named
перепечатка	reprint
переписка	correspondence
переплёт	binding, hard cover
перечень	list
периодический	periodical (adj.)
Пётр Великий	Tsar Peter I (the Great), 1672–1725
Петроград	Petrograd (until 1914 St. Petersburg, from 1924 Leningrad)

печатный	printed
печать	press; printing; print; seal, stamp
писатель	writer
писать	(ipfve) to write
письмо	letter
плакат	poster, wall sheet
планирование	planning
пленум	plenum, full meeting
по	(with acc.) up to
	(with dat.) because of, according to; along; ⎫ and many other meanings in set phrases ⎬
	(with loc.) after
повесть	tale, story
Поволжье	Volga region
повторно	again
под	(with acc.) under (motion)
	(with instr.) under, below (position)
подготовить	(pfve) to prepare. (-ся) to be prepared
подготовленный	prepared
поз. (= позиция)	item number
Политиздат	[name of publishing house – see 7.2.9]
полный	full
половина	half
положение	position; standing, situation; regulations
полутом	half-volume
получать	(ipfve), получить (pfve) to receive
польский	Polish
Польша	Poland
поправка	correction
посвящение	dedication
после	(with gen.) after
последний	last, latest
послесловие	postscript, afterword
пособие	textbook
почта	post (mail)

поэзия	poetry
поэт	poet
правда	truth
право	right(s); law
предисловие	preface, foreword
предмет	article, object; subject, topic
предметный указатель	subject index
председатель	chairman
прекращенный	ceased, discontinued
преподавание	teaching, instruction
при	(with loc.) at, in the time of, in the presence of
прикладной	applied
приложение	appendix, supplement
прим(еч). (= примечание)	note, comment
примечание	note, comment
природа	nature
про	(with acc.) about, concerning; for
проблема	problem
'Прогресс'	'Progress' Publishing House (see 7.2.9)
продолжать	(ipfve), продолжить (pfve) to continue. (-ся) to be continued
продолжающийся	continuing, serial (adj.)
продолжение	continuation, sequel
проза	prose
произведение	work, production
производство	production, manufacture
промышленность	industry
просвещение	education, enlightenment
'Просвещение'	'Education' Publishing House (see 7.2.9)
проспект	prospectus
против	(with gen.) against, opposite
Профиздат	[name of publishing house − see 7.2.9]
профсоюз (= профессио- нальный союз)	trade union
проч. (= прочий)	other
прочий	other

113

прочитать	(pfve) to read
публиковать	(ipfve) to publish. (-ся) to be published
публицистика	essay-writing (esp. on social and political matters), journalism
путеводитель	guide (-book)
путь	way, path, journey
пьеса	play (theatrical)
пятилетка	five-year plan
пятнадцать	fifteen
пятый	fifth
пять	five
пятьдесят	fifty
пятьсот	five hundred
р. (= рубль)	rouble
работа	work, activity
рабочий	working (adj.), worker (*ie* 'working person')
развивать	(ipfve), развить (pfve) to develop (transitive). (-ся) to develop (intransitive), to be developed
развивающийся	developing (adj.)
развитие	development
разговорник	phrase-book
разный	various, different
район	region, district, area
ранний	early
рассказ	story, tale
революция	revolution
ред. (= редактор)	editor
(= редакционный)	editorial (adj.)
(= редакция)	editorial staff; editorship
редактор	editor
редакционный	editorial (adj.)
редакция	editorial staff; editorship
редкий	rare

редколлегия (= редакционная коллегия)	editorial board
резюме	summary (often in another language)
рекомендательный	recommendatory, recommended
репродукция	reproduction
республика	republic
реферат	abstract; paper, essay
рецензия	review
речь	speech
решение	resolution
РЖ (= Реферативный журнал)	'Abstracts Journal' (see 4.1.11)
Рига	Riga (capital of the Latvian SSR)
Рим	Rome
рис. (= рисунок)	drawing
рисунок	drawing
РКП(б) (= Российская Коммунистическая партия (большевиков)	Russian Communist Party (Bolsheviks) (1919–1925)
рождение	birth
роль	role, part
роман	novel
российский	Russian (esp. applied to the pre-1917 Russian Empire)
Россия	Russia
РСДРП(б) (= Российская социал-демократичкая рабочая партия (большевиков)	Russian Social-Democratic Workers' Party (Bolsheviks) (1898–1918)
РСФСР	RSFSR, Russian Soviet Federal Socialist Republic (the largest of the 15 constituent republics of the USSR)
рубеж	border, boundary. за рубежом abroad
рубль	rouble
рукопись	manuscript
рус. (= русский)	Russian
русский	Russian (esp. applied to the Russian language and people)
Русь	Rus', (ancient) Russia

с, со	(with acc.) about, approximately
	(with gen.) from, off
	(with instr.) with
с. (= страница)	page
самый	most; the very . . .; same
Санктпетербург	St. Petersburg (1914—24 Petrograd, from 1924 Leningrad)
сборник	collection, symposium, volume of articles
сведение	information; (pl.) particulars
свет	world; light
сводный	combined, summary (adj.)
свой, своя, свое, свои	my (your, his, etc.) own, one's own
связь	connection, link; communications
'Связь'	'Communications' Publishing House (see 7.2.9)
север	north
северный	northern
седьмой	seventh
сельское хозяйство	agriculture
сельскохозяйственный	agricultural
семнадцать	seventeen
семь	seven
семьдесят	seventy
семья	family
сентябрь	September
середина	middle
серийный	serial (adj.)
серия	series
сессия	session, sitting
сибирский	Siberian
Сибирь	Siberia
система	system
сказание	story, legend
сказка	tale, story
славянский	Slavonic, Slavic
следовать	(ipfve) to follow

следующий	following
словарь	dictionary
словацкий	Slovak
слово	word
см. (= смотри)	see, refer to
(= сантиметр)	centimetre
смешанный	mixed
со	[variant of c]
собр. (= собрание)	collection
собрание	collection; gathering, meeting
совет	soviet, council
советский	Soviet (adj.)
'Советский композитор'	'Soviet Composer' Publishing House (see 7.2.9)
'Советский писатель'	'Soviet Writer' Publishing House (see 7.2.9)
совещание	conference, meeting
современный	contemporary
совхоз	sovkhoz, state farm
содержание	contents
созыв	convocation (*eg* of the Supreme Soviet)
сокр. (= сокращение)	abbreviation
(= сокращённый)	abbreviated
сообщение	report, information, communication
сорок	forty
сост. (= составитель)	compiler, writer
(= составленный)	compiled (by)
составитель	compiler, writer
составить	(pfve) to compile
сотрудник	collaborator
социальный	social
Соцэкгиз (= Госуд. изд-во социально-экономической литературы)	State Publishing House for Social and Economic Literature
соч. (= сочинение)	work, composition
сочинение	work, composition

союз	union
Спб. (= Санктпетербург)	St. Petersburg
список	list
справочник	handbook, guide
ср. (= сравни)	compare, cf.
сравнительный	comparative
среди	(with gen.) among, amidst
средний	middle (adj.)
СССР (= Союз Советских Социалистических Республик)	Union of Soviet Socialist Republics, USSR
ссылка	reference; exile, banishment
стандарт	standard
старый	old, ancient
статистика	statistics
'Статистика'	'Statistics' Publishing House
статья	article
стереотипный	stereotype(d)
стиль	style
стих	verse; (pl.) poetry
стихотворение	poem
сто	hundred
стоимость	cost, price, value
стол. (= столетие)	century
столетие	century
стр. (= страница)	page
страна	country, land
страница	page
строительство	building, construction
Стройиздат	[name of publishing house – see 7.2.9]
студент	student
США (= Соединённые Штаты Америки)	the USA
съезд	congress
т. (= том)	volume
таблица	table; plate (in book)

тадж. (= таджикский)	Tadzhik (adj.)
таджикский	Tadzhik (adj.)
Тадж ССР	Tadzhik SSR
так	so, thus
также	also, as well
Таллин	Tallinn (capital of Estonian SSR)
Ташкент	Tashkent (capital of Uzbek SSR)
Тбилиси	Tbilisi, Tiflis (capital of Georgian SSR)
твой, твоя, твое, твои	your(s)
творчество	creation, work
т.е. (= то есть)	that is, *ie*
театр	theatre
темплан (= тематический план)	long-term plan, plan of subjects (notably of publishing houses)
тетрадь	writing-book, copy-book; fascicule, part (of continuation)
техника	technology; technique
тип. (= типография)	printing house
типография	printing house
тираж	size of edition, number of copies
тит. л. (= титульный лист)	title page
титульный лист	title page
т.н. (= так называемый)	so-called
тоже	also, as well
только	only
том	volume
торговля	trade, commerce
тот, та, то, те	that
'Транспорт'	'Transport' Publishing House
третий	third (3rd)
треть	one-third (1/3)
три	three
тридцать	thirty
тринадцать	thirteen
триста	three hundred
труд	labour; (pl.) transactions

трудящийся	worker (declined as adj.)
ТССР	Turkmenian SSR
тт. (= тома)	volumes
турецкий	Turkish
туркм. (= туркменский)	Turkmenian, Turkmen
туркменский	Turkmenian, Turkmen
Турция	Turkey
ты	you (sing., familiar)
тыс. (= тысяча)	thousand
тысяча	thousand
у	(with gen.) by, at, near, in the possession of
уже	already
узб.. (= узбекский)	Uzbek
узбекский	Uzbek
Уз(б) ССР	Uzbek SSR
указатель	index
указать	(pfve) to show
указанный	shown
укр. (= украинский)	Ukrainian
Украина	the Ukraine
украинский	Ukrainian
ул. (= улица)	street
улица	street
университет	university
ун-т (= университет)	university
управление	administration, directorate
Урал	the Urals
урок	lesson
УССР	Ukrainian SSR (*not* the Union of Soviet Socialist Republics)
устав	statutes, regulations, charter
учебник	textbook, manual
учебный	educational, training (adj.)
учение	studies

учёный	learned, scholarly, scientific, academic
учёт	accounting
учитель	teacher
Учпедгиз (= Госуд. учебно-педагогическое изд-во)	State Educational Publishing House
февраль	February
физика	physics
физический	physical
'Физкультура и спорт'	'Physical Culture and Sport' Publishing House
Физматгиз (= Госуд. изд-во физико-математической литературы)	State Publishing House for Physics and Mathematical Literature
филиал	branch (*eg* of an institution or library)
филология	philology; literary and linguistic studies
финансы	finance
'Финансы'	'Finance' Publishing House
фирма	firm
фольклор	folklore
фонд	stock; (in library or archives) holdings, collection
фр. (= французский)	French
Франция	France
французский	French
ФРГ	Federal Republic of Germany (West Germany)
Фрунзе	Frunze (capital of the Kirghiz SSR)
фунт	pound
характер	character, nature
химия	chemistry
'Химия'	'Chemistry' Publishing House (see 7.2.9)
хозяйство	economy; sector of the economy
хороший	good
хрестоматия	collection of readings

'Художественная литература'	'Literature' Publishing House (see 7.2.9)
художественный	artistic, to do with the arts
художник	artist, designer
ц. (= цена)	price
царь	tsar
целый	whole, full. в целом as a whole
цена	price
центральный	central
церковь	church
цифра	figure
ЦК (= Центральный комитет)	Central Committee
ч. (= часть)	part, section
часть	part, section
человек	person, man
через	(with acc.) over, across, through
Чёрное море	Black Sea
черт. (= чертёж)	drawing, draft
чертёж	drawing, draft
четверть	quarter
четвёртый	fourth
четыре	four
четыреста	four hundred
четырнадцать	fourteen
Чехословакия	Czechoslovakia
чешский	Czech, Bohemian
читатель	reader
читать	(ipfve) to read
член	member
что	what
шестнадцать	sixteen
шестой	sixth
шесть	six
шестьдесят	sixty

школа	school. высшая школа higher school (*ie* university)
ЭВМ (= электронная вычислительная машина)	computer
экз. (= экземпляр)	copy, specimen
экземпляр	copy, specimen
экономика	economics, economic structure
'Экономика'	'Economics' Publishing House
экономия	economy
энергетика	power (production and industry)
'Энергия'	'Energy' Publishing House (see 7.2.9)
энциклопедия	encyclopedia
эпоха	epoch, age
эра	era
ЭССР	Estonian SSR
эст. (= эстонский)	Estonian
эстонский	Estonian
этика	ethics
этот, эта, это, эти	this
юг	south
южный	southern
'Юридическая литература'	'Legal Literature' Publishing House
юридический	legal, juridical
я	I
яз. (= язык)	language
язык	language
языкознание	linguistics
январь	January

INDEX

References are to section number